A Walk

through Parenting

Create Your Personal Parenting Plan

Ruth Ann Brinkmann, PhD

ISBN-10:   1477675051

EAN-13:   9781477675052

Library of Congress Control Number: 2012911237
CreateSpace Independent Publishing Platform
North Charleston, South Carolina

This book is dedicated to

To my parents,
Ruth and Winnie Uhrig,
who loved me so I could love my children.

To my co-parent,
Erwin H. Brinkmann, PhD,
who brought insight to the parenting process.

To our children,
Ron, Tim, and Sheri,
who taught me how to be a parent.

To my grandchildren,
Alex, Aundrea, Alyssa, Rachel, Anna, and Josh
who make the future look bright.

Acknowledgments

This book probably would not have been written, especially in this way, had it not been for the parenting groups I was privileged to serve. I thank the Mothers of Preschoolers (MOPS) groups that met at Trinity Lutheran Church in Edwardsville, Illinois. You kept me current on parenting concerns and suggested I write a parenting book. I thank all of the foster and adoptive parents who attended the Lutheran Child and Family Services of Illinois workshops at which I was a presenter. Your questions and input increased my conviction that parenting plans had to be individualized.

Every parent knows that having children causes one to rethink how to parent. Ron, Tim, and Sheri, you helped shape my understanding of parenting. I love being your mom! You are the greatest!

My heartfelt thanks goes to my son, Ron Brinkmann, who read and reread my manuscript as it went through a total metamorphosis. I am so grateful to my daughter-in-law, Karen Brinkmann, for being my go-to person when I had questions regarding my manuscript. Thanks to my daughter, Sheri Loeffelman, to Sandra Knight, and a special thanks to Catherine Fullerton for providing the viewpoint of a first-time parent-to-be. Thanks to Diane Gebhardt, who gave up time on the Florida beach to proofread my book and a special shout-out to my colleague and friend, Fredna Scroggins, PhD, for her valuable feedback.

You, my beloved grandchildren, - Alex, Aundrea, Alyssa, and Anna Loeffelman, and Rachel and Josh Brinkmann - make my heart sing. A special thanks to my book's artists, Anna, Aundrea, Rachel and Josh.

Contents

A Walk Through Parenting
Create Your Personal Parenting Plan

Introduction

Come. Walk with me through parenting. Our exploration of parenting will be like taking a walk through a magnificent garden accompanied by a master gardener. As the two of you explore the various paths that wind through an array of plants, your companion explains why some plants are growing and becoming objects of beauty while others are withering and dying. She helps you avoid the rose thorns that try to snag you. As you walk along a path, you gather the flowers that are most appealing to you. You leave with a bouquet that is uniquely yours. As you exit the garden, you find yourself filled with the confidence that future walks through this and other gardens will be more enjoyable because of your new knowledge.

Think of me as your personal guide and this book as a series of paths through parenting. Together we will explore paths that will sharpen your understanding of your child from birth through the elementary grades. I will help you avoid the thorns of parenting. I will give you a variety of parenting techniques and explain when and how to use them. You will learn that no one technique solves all parenting challenges. Therefore you will select, from an array of parenting techniques, the ones that meld with your values and are appropriate for your child. You will complete the book with a parenting plan that is uniquely yours and filled with the confidence that, because of our walk together, your parenting experiences will become easier and more enjoyable.

Keep this book handy, as it will be a valuable resource as your child grows. What worked well with your preschooler may be much less effective when your child is in elementary school. As your child's thinking and needs change, so should your parenting plan.

Let's take a brief look at the parenting paths we'll walk:

PATH 1   will guide you through self-reflection and will enable you to determine the kind of parent you want to be.

PATH 2   will let you discover why you, as a parent, have so much influence on your child.

PATH 3   will teach you how to adjust your parenting based on your child's individuality.

PATH 4   will teach you how to adjust your parenting based on your child's level of development from birth through age twelve.

PATH 5   will teach you how to anticipate and reduce parenting problems.

PATH 6   will teach you how to use positive parenting and why it is powerful parenting.

PATH 7   will teach you how to keep your child's inappropriate behaviors from escalating.

PATH 8   will provide you appropriate responses to your child's inappropriate behaviors.

PATH 9   will teach you how to develop your child's self-control.

PATH 10 will help you prepare your child for the world beyond your home.

PATH 11 will help you avoid the obstacles that clutter the paths through parenting.

PATH 12 will help you finalize your parenting plan.

Come. Let's start our walk down the parenting paths.

Artwork by Rachel

Path 1

Examine Your Present Parenting

I hope you are as anxious to start our walk through parenting as I am. On this path I will ask you to reflect on the skills and beliefs you bring to the parenting process and the skills you want to possess at the completion of our walk through parenting.

Unlike most parenting books, this one will not tell you to follow a specific approach to parenting. Instead, I will discuss the strengths and weaknesses of various parenting techniques and ask you to select those that work for you and your child.

This does not mean there are no boundaries. You absolutely must never degrade your child, inflict emotional pain, or use physical punishment. Spanking and screaming are out; they are nothing but parental temper tantrums.

Just as there are things you must not do, there are things you must do. The most important absolute of good parenting is love. Your love will be the fountain of energy needed for consistency—and no parenting approach will work unless you administer it consistently.

Know Yourself

Know who you are now

You are unique. You approach challenges and opportunities differently than your co-parent does. You approach parenting with a method similar to how you approach other situations in your life. Do you tend to reflect on things and respond thoughtfully? If so, you will probably pause before you act and will be drawn to techniques that teach problem solving. Or are you quick to react? If you get mad quickly, be honest with yourself and select parenting techniques that give you a chance to calm down before you speak. When you get to Path 3 and start reflecting on your child's temperament, reflect on yours also. While temperament tends to be stable across situations and time, it can be modified, and you may need to modify your temperament for the welfare of your child.

A warning to the quiet, laid-back parent: If you are quiet or want to always give your child options, you may shun the more controlling approaches. But if your child needs greater control because of the current situation, his temperament, or special needs, and you fail to provide it, you will soon find yourself facing an out-of-control child. One friend, reflecting on the parenting problems plaguing a mutual acquaintance, said, "She is just too nice to her children." No, she was not actually being "too nice." Rather, she was not modifying her temperament to meet the needs of her children. The children did whatever pleased them and, as a result, developed many inappropriate behaviors. She ignored these behaviors because she disliked confrontations. If you find that your child—not you—is the one who controls what goes on in your home, and you want a remedy, you can select several of the controlling approaches that require minimal confrontation. If used consistently, they will help you regain control. You are not being mean. You are just being the parent.

If you think ignoring irritating behaviors is an act of kindness, read the section titled "Your child deserves to be liked" found on Path 5. If you give in to your child because you dislike verbal confrontations, you may be more comfortable using nonverbal instructions, such as posting a weekly chart that lists her tasks. For the sake of your child, you must gain control of your home. To do so, you must select parenting techniques, set clear guidelines, and consistently enforce them. You are the adult. Act like it.

A warning to the highly controlling parent: An unnecessarily high level of control can also create problems. It can cause your child to rebel or to withdraw. Even if you prefer the more controlling techniques, you need to learn how to use the freedom-within-limits approaches described along Path 9. You will need those approaches to develop your child's self-control and decision-making skills. Your child will need opportunities to learn from his own mistakes without your lecturing him. If you are highly controlling in other areas of your life, you will need to modify your temperament to allow your child freedom, within the limits you set, in order for him to develop his interests and abilities. Just as a balanced meal consists of a variety of foods, balanced parenting requires both controlling and freedom-within-limits approaches.

Know your expectations

Your expectations, which must be appropriate for the developmental level of your child (see Path 4), will be affected by your interests and your values.

Families have various interests: which ones do you encourage? Sports? Music? Art? Reading? Expecting your child to excel in your chief area of interest can be a recipe for disaster. On the other hand, if you include your child when you are enjoying your interests, you will expand her view of the world and her options.

Your values, which grow out of your experiences, your culture, and your religious beliefs, determine the rules you establish for your child and the behaviors you model.

What personal characteristics do you value? Neat and organized, or creative and spontaneous? Does your culture stress setting aside personal goals for the good of the group or independence? While there are variations within all cultural groups, your culture does influence the goals you have for your child.

Your view on religion will also influence your values. If your life is rooted in a faith, the teachings of your religion will permeate your values. As a Christian, I tried to model a Christ-centered life.

Select five to ten life-guiding principles that reflect your values and can be applied to many situations. This is more effective than creating a hundred specific rules for your child. Teach your child how to apply those life guides to the everyday events of life. For example, I had seven life guides:

1. Love God.
2. Respect yourself.
3. Respect others.

4. Respect the environment.
5. Contribute to the welfare of others.
6. Think and make good decisions.
7. Set goals and strive to reach them.

My children can apply these life guides to many situations. For example, loving God promotes church attendance and provides each family member the comfort that comes from knowing the love of God. Self-respect encourages using words to express wants, getting adequate sleep, and selecting healthy foods. Respecting others includes developing empathy, learning to share, using polite rather than abrasive words, and expressing feelings verbally rather than physically. Respecting the environment covers keeping one's room orderly and not littering. Contributing to the welfare of others includes doing chores such as setting the table and volunteer work (carefully chosen for the child's age), such as collecting canned goods to give to the local food pantry. Thinking and making good decisions requires a child to explain how his decisions affect him and others. Setting goals and striving to reach them includes saving money to buy a toy and setting a time to finish chores.

Rules are the natural outcome of—and should flow from—your life guides. For example, there are several rules that could flow from the life guide of respecting the environment:

- Pick up your toys.
- Hang up your coat when you come inside.
- Clear your place at the table.
- Put your dishes in the dishwasher.

While your life guides and rules will be different from mine, you do need to establish them. Rules that flow from life guides will seem less arbitrary. For example, when you say, "You have to pick up your

life - other people.   ④ Help others. ⑤ Complete what you start
⑥ Love nature

ıothes, because our family respects the environment," you are teaching your child how to apply your values to an everyday decision. As your child questions your rules, you will have many opportunities to restate your life guides and thus teach your values. Teaching values is vital to raising a competent child.

Know how you got here

Most people parent the way they were parented. Think of how often you hear something along the lines of "That's how my parents did it, and I turned out OK." To reject the way one was parented is almost paramount to saying, "I'm not OK," but the decision to not follow your parents' parenting style is neither self-rejection nor parent rejection! Yes, you turned out great, but there are other ways that may work as well or even better. You don't drive the same car your parents drove, nor do you insist on the same hairstyle, so why should you parent like your parents?

Other people are determined *not* to parent like they were parented. Adults raised in a dysfunctional home lack a model for appropriate parenting. In his book *A Man Called Dave*, Dave Pelzer describes his childhood abuse. He said he knew what not to do but had no idea what a parent *should* do. If you came from a dysfunctional family and observed only inappropriate parenting, carefully read the reasons for, and the times to use, each of the parenting approaches described.

It is counterproductive to reject (or defend) any given parenting approach just because your parent or parents used it. Examine the approaches in this book and ask yourself if they will help you reach your goals.

Artwork by Aundrea

Decide What Kind of Parent You Want to Become

Expect to change your parenting style

A frequently quoted lighthearted definition of insanity is the behavior of doing the same thing repeatedly yet expecting different results. If you want your child's behavior to change, expect to change your parenting behavior!

You can yell at your child and demand she change, but that will probably not get the results you want. Instead, it will probably increase the likelihood that your child will scream at you and others. Good parenting requires you to discover what you are doing that contributes to your child's present behavior. The trick to changing your child's behavior is changing what *you* do. You may need to:

- Change how you *talk* to your child;
- Change how you *react* to your child's behavior;

- Create an *environment* that enables your child to succeed;
- Change the *expectations* you have for your child.

As you continue reading this book, you will discover some changes you can make in your parenting that will benefit your child.

Consider the consequences of your parenting style

Diane Baumrind, a well-respected psychologist in the field of mental health, defines four parenting styles: authoritarian, authoritative, indulgent/passive, and uninvolved. Each has a distinctly different effect on the child.

Authoritarian

Authoritarian parents value immediate and total obedience. Rules are selected based on the needs of the adults. They are inflexible and harsh. The parents feel it is their job to instill obedience. They have strict rules and maintain firm control of the child's behavior. They mete out punishment for infractions of the rules without factoring in the needs of their child. Children are expected to obey without question. This type of parenting creates a child who is either extremely submissive or, especially when the parent is not around, very rebellious. Control of the child's behavior is primarily external.

Authoritative

While authoritative parents have firm rules and enforce them, they also consider the feelings and needs of the children. The parents don't permit the children to manipulate them but do allow their children to express individuality. Rules are designed to promote self-control and an understanding of how the rules benefit the children themselves, the family, and society as a whole. Authoritative parenting has been found to reduce the likelihood that adolescents become involved in risky behaviors such as smoking and sexual promiscuity. Children raised by authoritative parents develop self-control and score high on measures of social competency and academic success.

Indulgent/Passive

Indulgent/passive parents don't want to inhibit their children's creativity or independence and therefore set few or no rules. They encourage their children to do as they please. These parents often give their children a great deal of love and attention but fail to set firm limits. These children become self-centered and score low on social competency and academic success.

Uninvolved

Uninvolved parents feel they should not influence their children's direction of development. Their goal is to let their children evolve into the people they are "meant" to become. They don't expect much from their children. While their goal is to avoid impacting natural development and determining the future of their children, in reality the impact of this approach is as great as the preceding approaches. These children measure the lowest in academic success, social skills, and motivation.

While there are many choices you can make and still be a good parent, your overall style isn't one of them. The authoritarian, the indulgent/passive, and the uninvolved styles will cause you problems and will hurt your child's development. It is important to be authoritative. You must set limits and select parenting *techniques* based on the needs of the child and family.

Consider the consequences of your present parenting techniques

Your parenting techniques—the specific approaches you use to manage your child's day-to-day behavior—range from punitive to positive. In the early years of our country, parents were advised not to spare the rod, as that would spoil the child. However, studies show that physical punishment and verbal tirades have a detrimental effect on children. They:

- Introduce the element of fear, and fear can inhibit the development of a positive parent-child relationship;
- Can destroy your child's spirit (reduce self-worth) or make your child angry and rebellious, depending on your child's temperament;
- Model violence, and children are inclined to do what is modeled.

Punishment, which is inflicting physical or emotional pain to stop a behavior, identifies the behavior you don't want but fails to identify the behavior you *do* want. You still have to teach your child what to do instead of the undesired behavior. Skip the pain and go directly to teaching the behaviors you want your child to develop by using alternative parenting techniques.

I am certain that you can name a child—maybe yourself—who was spanked and is neither withdrawn nor aggressive. Like the side effects of a medicine, side effects to punishment can vary depending on the individual as well as the strength, frequency, and duration of the punishment. Many medications have been withdrawn from the market because of side effects, and not everyone who took that medication ended up suffering the maximum, or even any, negative effects. Nevertheless, we want those medications replaced with others that enable us to get well without the fear of harmful side effects. Physical punishment, with its known side effects, needs to be replaced with positive parenting techniques.

Seek Parenting Information

An empty barrel makes more noise than a full one

Just as an empty barrel makes more noise than a full one, parents without lots of parenting options tend to resort to the two *s*'s—screaming and spanking. Don't be like the noisy, empty barrel; develop a full repertoire of parenting techniques.

Dr. Dodson, in his book *How to Father*, reports that parents often resort to punishment because they lack information about effective ways to discipline. Parents unfamiliar with the multitude of available techniques often conclude that the only alternative to spanking is to let children do whatever they want. This book provides many alternatives. In fact, the alternatives to spanking and screaming are so numerous that it took me five paths (Paths 5 through 9) to cover them! You do not need to be an empty barrel that makes a lot of noise. You will have many options, which will enable you to select techniques best suited to you and your child and to create a comprehensive parenting plan.

Select parenting techniques wisely

Your child lacks the wisdom, experience, and thinking skills necessary to run your home. A child's brain is just not developed enough to make decisions that require complex thinking. Path 4, which explores the stages of child development, will show you how your child's age-typical thinking can lead her to conclusions adults would consider illogical. Unlike your child, you have the ability to think *abstractly* and to mentally manipulate possible solutions. You will use those adult thinking skills to actively consider various parenting techniques. You will:

- *Compare* several approaches and consider their similarities and differences;
- *Reject* the techniques that do not meet your child's needs;
- *Select* the ones most valuable to your child;
- <u>Combine</u> two or more of the techniques.

After *comparing* two or more techniques, you may conclude that only one of them is appropriate in a specific situation. For example (as discussed in Path 8) you may need to decide whether recognizing a behavior or ignoring it should be used for a specific incident. Since these two approaches require *directly opposing parenting actions* and are *appropriate in totally different situations*, you will need to decide which one fits your particular situation.

There will be times where you will *reject* approaches because they will not work with your child due to age or temperament. For example, if your child has a tendency to be passive and to sulk when things go wrong, you may reject time-out, because it enables her to go off by herself and sulk. You may conclude that time-out encourages passive actions instead of active ones, and your child already leans too heavily in that direction. Thus, you may conclude that you will not use time-out with her but will look for another approach.

You will also *select* parenting techniques. For example, you may select approaches based on the age of your child. You may decide that time-out will work well with your two-year-old and that conflict resolution is exactly what your ten-year-old needs.

There may be times when you *reject* an approach for one of your children but *select* it for your other child. You may find that the more verbal approach works well with one of your children but not with the other. One family found that one of their children cooperated if he understood the reason for their decision; therefore, with him, they used techniques that included verbal interaction. The other child viewed an explanation as an invitation to argue; therefore, the parent used techniques that require little or no talking.

On some occasions you will find it useful to *combine* approaches. For example, you could combine being consistent, which is discussed on Path 5, with developing a plan to teach your rules, which is discussed on Path 6. Also, after reading what Path 5 says about consistency and flexibility and how they support each other, you may decide to combine them. While each technique needs to be explained separately, in parenting you may find it useful to combine some of them as a way to increase the effectiveness of both of them.

As you go down the paths of parenting, keeping your child's needs foremost in your mind, take an honest, introspective look at yourself and decide if you need to modify your present parenting.

Create a Functional Family

Find a parent/parent solution

If you have not already done so, at this time tell your co-parent about this book and its goal of helping you create a unified parenting plan. Urge your co-parent to read this book. If that does not occur, you can at least share what you are learning. Parenting is easier and definitely more fun when co-parents cooperate. If you don't cooperate with each other, your child, who is perceptive, will use your disagreements to her advantage. A child whose parents share a common parenting plan is indeed fortunate.

I have provided you with information that can deepen your understanding of your child and yourself. You will need this knowledge to develop a professionally based, *unified* approach to parenting. The closer you can come to an agreement, the better for the child. Both of you will likely need to make changes to create the home environment and parenting plan you desire.

This book provides information the two of you can use to create a combined parenting plan appropriate for your child. Going through this book together can provide the structure and the information that will assist you in developing a unified plan. If communication breaks down, seek a parent coach or family counselor to walk you through the book.

Consider the needs of your child

A functional family respects each person's unique needs and interests. On the next Path we are focusing on recognizing and meeting the needs of each of your children. If your family consists of children of various ages, consider, with your co-parent, how you will use your life guides to fit their age-based needs. For example, both your four-year-old and your eleven-year-old need to take care of their health (life guide), but the amount of sleep each needs is not the same. While having a life guide may not prevent the younger child from proclaiming "unfair" when he has to go to bed before the older sibling, it will provide the basis for discussing your age-based expectations. If your child is going from one parent's home to the other parent's home, having a common rule will make life easier for your child and for both parents.

Consider how a technique is working with your child. After such a discussion, one set of parents concluded that sending their sons to their room was not working, as one would happily find something to read and the other would take a desired nap. They decided that it would be better to have them sit in a chair, because both boys found that boring. Since it was boring, it served as a deterrent. If a technique isn't working, don't blame yourself or give up; try another technique.

Path 2

Relax, You Are the Right Person for the Job!

The adoption agency finally called. We could pick up our baby. As we headed home, my heart raced with excitement, but with each mile, doubts about my parenting skills grew. My husband's voice broke the silence: "I hope you know what to do with this baby." The panic in my husband's voice increased the uncertainties I felt. "We have everything we need," I said with all the assurance I could muster. Then I prayed that God would help our baby survive me. Our baby didn't just survive: he thrived. As I studied child psychology, I learned that we, as parents, are the most influential people in our child's life because we:

- Are the first people in our child's life (primacy);
- Are with our child over a longer timeline than any other person (duration);

- Bond (connect) emotionally with our child;
- Have a unique love commitment to our child.

Primacy, duration, bonding, and love give you, the parent, more influence on your child than anyone else. Relax. God has designed you and your child for success.

Primacy: You Are Number One

Primacy refers to your position as the first person in a sequence of influences. Because you are the first influence, you also become the major influence. Reflect on how you got ready for an important interview. Did you carefully select what to wear and plan what to say? Probably. After all, you never get a second chance to make a first impression. *The first impression creates the standard for future evaluations and is resistant to change.*

You are the first person in your child's life; therefore, your child's first impression of the world is based on your interactions with him. For example, your child will decide, based on his contact with you, whether people are kind and trustworthy or unkind and undependable.

You, as a parent, are the first to interpret the world for your child. You are the first to introduce values and beliefs. These early experiences will create the standards he will use to evaluate all future experiences. Yes, the television, the neighbor, the teacher, and peers will enter your child's life and convey new values. He may try them and engage in behavior you do not want. Use those times to reteach your values and your behavioral expectations. Your child will not be a copy of you. But he will use the values you portray to evaluate the values of other people. Live your values, and your child will reflect them to the world. However, if you say one thing but do another, your child will do what you do, rather than what you say. You—for good or for bad—are your child's primary and, therefore, most powerful influence.

Duration: Time Is on Your Side

Duration refers to the *cumulative* time that you are parenting, starting with the first time you held your child until he is totally independent. While these hours are not sequential, your *total number of hours* is extensive, because they are accumulated *across an extended timeline.* You have time to make your expectations permanent.

For example, you may have heard that once you learn to ride a bike, you will never forget. This may well be true because, as illustrated below, learning to ride a bike incorporates all four of the conditions needed to make learning permanent:

1. The *total number of hours* spent learning the task must be extensive enough for the learner to do the task automatically. In the case of the bike rider, the number of hours available must be enough for him to learn how to ride the bike without thinking

about the separate skills needed for success—in other words, automation.

2. The *hours* spent learning must be *spread across an extended timeline*. The total number of hours does not occur in a short time span; bike riding is spread across many years.

3. The skill must be *practiced correctly*. To ride a bike without falling, the rider is forced to use all the skills, such as maintaining balance and using the gears, correctly.

4. The skill *continues* to be practiced *until it becomes automatic* (that is, done without thinking). A successful bike rider no longer has to think about how to pedal or balance. It becomes an automatic skill.

Let's look at why *you* are the ideal person to make your child's learning permanent.

Learning takes hours and hours of time

The total number of hours you spend with your child over your parenting years is extensive. Some days you will spend just a few hours together; other days, eighteen hours. If you add all the hours each day, seven days a week, fifty-two weeks a year for eighteen or more years, I am sure you will come up with a huge number. You have hours and hours with your child, and learning takes time. For example, the *total* number of hours spent picking up clothes is very high; therefore, if you make certain your child picks up her clothes at home, she will probably continue to do so when she leaves. You have created a habit. If you don't require picking up clothes, your child will acquire the habit of dropping clothes where she takes them off, and that will become a habit. Either way, it will be a hard habit to break, because the *total number of hours* engaged in that activity was extensive.

Learning requires repetition spread over time

A habit isn't acquired in one act, nor is it mastered in a single sitting; it must be done week after week, year after year. Just as bike riding is fine-tuned over the course of years, your child's values and behaviors, such as picking up—or not picking up—her clothes will be developed and refined over a long stretch of time. Since parenting stretches over many years, you have this type of time.

Learning requires correct practice

Every time you rode your bike without falling, you practiced it correctly. If you have ever practiced something incorrectly, such as a piece of music, you know that learning it incorrectly just increases the difficulty of learning it correctly. What is practiced, whether correct or incorrect, becomes permanent.

Therefore, if you tell your child to pick up his clothes—but then do it for him—he will learn to leave his clothes where they drop. That is what he will practice. If your child practices folding and storing clean clothes and putting all dirty clothes inside a hamper, that behavior is practice and will, therefore, become automatic. You determine what your child practices and, therefore, what becomes permanent. It is important to remember that practice does not make perfect. Practice makes permanent.

Duration enables skills and behaviors to become automatic

When your child practices a skill or a behavior long enough, she stops thinking about it. By the time she is on her own, she will automatically pick up her clothes or will automatically scatter them everywhere without analyzing what she's doing.

Duration is what makes the modeling of behavior so powerful. Your child's observations are spread over a long timeline. She tries doing what she sees you do (practices by role-playing) and eventually follows your example automatically. If you want to know how your child perceives you, just listen to what she is saying when she is playing with a toy or talking to a friend. She will be doing and saying what she sees you do and hears you say. Do you ever find yourself doing something just like your parent? Was it something taught or "caught" through observations?

These four principles of learning apply not only to the taught behaviors discussed previously, but also to the behaviors you model. The time your child spends observing you is extensive because it is spread across the entire time your children lives in your home. He will copy your behaviors (practice it) until the behaviors become automatic. Is your child, as he follows your example, practicing a behavior you hope will become a permanent habit? If so, great. If not, you need to model the behaviors and values you want your child to develop. Values, such as how you treat others, take a great deal of observation and practice. Your child will, in time, automatically integrate the values you demonstrate. If you scream at, or demean, a family member, your child will practice that behavior and will learn to scream at and demean others. If you show love and respect, your child will show love and respect to others and to you. Values are developed as a child mimics (practices) what he sees you do.

While it is important to remember that you are the most influential person in your child's life, it is also important to remember that your child is not a blank slate you can write on to create the child of your dreams; he comes with inborn tendencies. Neither can you totally insulate him from the culture in which you live. Thus, you may wonder how much influence others have on your child. For comparison, consider how long you remembered the information you studied for a specific test or course. It probably was not for very long. You learned the information, used it to answer questions, and then moved on to other things. Learning from other people who have only a year or so to influence your child is like cramming for a test. For a year or so, your child will use what he learned, but in most cases, your child will move on when that relationship is over. The principles of learning work to your advantage. What *you* model and teach will last a lifetime. Yes, there are other forces at work creating this unique individual that is your child, but of all these influences, you are the single most powerful influence.

Bonding: Emotions Are Memory Magnets

"Can't you see what needs to be done?" my exasperated mother complained. To this day, when I am in a kitchen with other women, I hear the annoyance in my mother's voice and immediately look for ways to help. I certainly can't just stand and visit. I must get busy. My mother goes with me wherever I go.

This lasting influence occurred because of the *bond*—the two-way emotional connection—I have with my mother. Just as glue can bond two items together, a child and his parents are bonded in a way unlike any other human relationship. The impact that bonding with your infant will have on the development of your child is discussed on Path 4. On this path I will discuss how this bonding increases the influence you have on your child. Think about your childhood. Reflect on an event from your early years. Is there an emotional element to the specific event you remembered? Most likely. Our emotions are memory magnets.

I'm sure you remember times when you got in trouble. Does your mother's or father's reprimand from your childhood still affect your behavior? What behaviors did your parents praise? Do you feel you are worthwhile when you do those behaviors?

The fact that our parents live within us is not bad if they instilled commitment to honesty, concern for others, and other socially appropriate behaviors. Just as you incorporate your parents' standards into your value system, your children will incorporate your values because of the emotional connection you have with him. Children who live in an emotionally dysfunctional home carry those emotional scars into adulthood. Children love and seek the parent even when the parent is abusive. Since emotions increase memory, it is very, very important that your child's experiences are rooted in loving relationships.

During times of need, people become more dependent and more easily influenced. You are the one who meets your child's needs. When your child is sick, skins her knee, or is afraid of the monster under the bed, she calls you. You are the one who makes her feel better. Because you are there in her time of need, trust develops. Because of this trust, you become influential. For better or for worse, you are powerful. Use this power for the benefit of your child.

Love: The Foundation of Parenting

Love is the strong emotional outpouring of feeling you have for another person. It is essential for good parenting. Your love for your child will fuel your commitment and give you the energy you will need to be a good parent. Love is what will get you up out of a chair and away from the television to make certain your child is following your instructions. Love is what will get you to put down your cell phone and talk to her. When you are tired and stressed by life, love will create that last burst of energy required to meet the challenges of parenting. Love is what lets you set aside your personal interests to encourage her to pursue her interests. It puts a knot in your stomach and makes every nerve in your body jingle when she is pitching in a little league game or competing in a music competition. When your child moves into adulthood, love is what enables you to let your child go and let him create his own life.

Of course, love doesn't always look the same. Your child will have her preferred ways of expressing and receiving love. The age and temperament of your child will determine how she wants you to express your love and how she will express her love for you.

SCENARIO

Thoughts of my children flooded my heart as I flew home from a professional meeting. Walking into the terminal, I quickly spotted my husband and our three children waiting for me. Our daughter, age five, was in front of her dad, arms up. Our two sons, ages seven and nine, were a few steps behind their dad and standing sideways, looking as if they were ready to sprint in the opposite direction. I kissed my daughter and husband and then, without moving toward them, I verbally greeted my two sons and told them how glad I was to see them. When I got to the car, each boy gave me a hug and kiss. I commented, "You looked like you were ready to run if I tried to kiss you in the airport."

My nine-year-old responded, "No need to make a scene in public."

Expressing love through physical contact, such as touching, hugging, and kissing, is just one of the ways you can show love. But, as the previous scenario demonstrates, you also need other ways to show your love. Your child may prefer praise, going places together, or working together on a project. Observe your child to determine what draws the two of you closer together. Remember, love is an essential, not a luxury.

As you go forth, remember that primacy (being the first and most influential person), duration (having the longest and most time), bonding (the emotional "glue" or two-way connection with your child), and love (your outpouring of affection toward your child) ensure that you will be the most influential person in your child's life.

Path 3

Discover Your Child's Uniqueness

Your child is unique! The genetics he received from his parents reach back generations and combine to create a one of-a-kind person. In addition, his environment—composed of many distinctive elements—interacts in a dynamic way with these inborn characteristics. This environment includes your own interests and temperament, your child's place in your family (oldest, middle, or youngest), your extended family, and your friends and the community in which you live. All in all, your child will become someone who has never existed before.

Welcome Your Unique Child

I don't know what kind of child you were expecting, but I am positive you had some surprises. Your child is not like a hunk of clay that you can molded into the child of your dreams. He was born with a distinct personality and temperament. He has his own level of curiosity and interest in adventure. The speed at which he achieves developmental milestones is different from other babies.

I was surprised at how different my babies were from the very beginning. Our first son loved to be held tightly while our second son wanted to be held loosely so he could move and exercise his arms and legs. Our daughter lay calmly in my arms. My first child did not, as I had expected, teach me what to expect of my subsequent children.

Your child is not a miniature of yourself. Oh, she may have characteristics like yours or your co-parent's, but her genetics have come together in a unique way. Parenting is like unwrapping a wonderful present. Your role as a parent is to discover your real child.

Discover Your Child's Temperament

One way people differ from each other is temperament. Temperament, which is inborn, is how an individual approaches the world. The interaction of your temperament with your child's temperament will either make your child's life and your parenting easier or more difficult. Your reflex response to your child will be greatly influenced by your temperament, and your child's response to your parenting technique will be greatly influenced by his temperament. While there are various ways of categorizing temperament, the following one, originated by Herbert Birch and further developed by Thomas and Chess, is one of the more commonly used. I have identified the various temperaments and described the behaviors of a person who ranks low as well as the behaviors of a person who ranks high in each of the temperaments. After reading the descriptions of behaviors, decide whether your child ranks low or high in each of them. Carefully consider how your child's ranking will affect your selection of parenting techniques.

Description of Temperaments and Their Effect on Parenting

Activity Level (general physical activity) *high*

The highly active child is constantly moving, running, and jumping. He finds it hard to sit still at home or school, making parenting more difficult. The less active child often prefers drawing, doing puzzles, and reading, which gives his parent more quiet time, making parenting easier.

Regularity (predictability of biological factors) *?.*

If your child eats, sleeps, and has bowel movements at predictable times, he has high regularity and is also more likely to accept your family schedule. This can make parenting easier. If your child eats, sleeps, and defecates at random times each day, he has low regularity and will probably also resist your attempts to have him adjust to your schedule, making parenting more difficult. On the other hand, if you and your child are both regular or both irregular, parenting will be easier.

Distractibility (reaction to the task) *Low*

The child with high distractibility is unable to concentrate if the activity does not interest her, unlikely to return to a task when interrupted, and likely to have one or more uncompleted projects. This makes parenting harder. The child with low distractibility will concentrate on the task even if it does not interest her, will return to a task when interrupted, and will complete most tasks. This makes parenting easier.

Sensory Threshold (reaction to sensory stimuli)   *Low*

The child with a high sensory threshold is distracted and bothered by noise, lights, smells, and textures. This makes parenting harder. On the other hand, the child with a low sensory threshold is able to maintain focus despite external sensory distractions. This makes parenting easier.

Approach/Withdrawal (initial response to situations or strangers)   *Bolder*

The bold child approaches new people and situations without hesitation while the withdrawn child is shy, stands back, and watches before approaching the situation or person. Either extreme can make parenting more difficult. A middle reaction makes parenting easier.

Adaptability (length of time needed to change)   *Quick*

This refers to the length of time it takes the child to adjust to change (not the child's original reaction). The "easy" child will adjust quickly to a new school or schedule, while a resistant child may take a long time. The quick-to-adjust child makes parenting easier, while the child who takes a long time to adjust makes parenting more difficult.

Persistence (unwilling to give up)   *persistent*

The persistent child does not give up easily. Once he starts something, he continues, in spite of interventions. Thus, he is willing to work on a task even in the face of frustration. If it is a parent-approved task, persistence makes parenting easier. On the other hand, he also refuses to stop an activity (e.g., come when called for a meal or stop playing ball). This makes it hard to redirect or stop his behavior once it starts.

Mood (prevailing emotional state)

A child's prevailing emotional state shows up early in the baby's tendency to smile and coo or cry and fuss. While a child is biologically wired to be primarily happy or unhappy, all children demonstrate an array of emotions from joy to sorrow. Many factors, including health, can temporarily influence the mood of an infant or child. A fussy, whiny child makes parenting difficult, while a child who is primarily happy makes parenting easier.

Intensity (the strength of the child's response)

The child with high intensity laughs, screams, or cries loudly. She jumps for joy and laughs boldly or reacts violently and defiantly, depending on her mood. The child with low intensity gives a slight smile or may not openly show her feelings. A child with moderate intensity is easier to parent than a child with either very high or very low intensity.

Knowing your child's temperament can help you anticipate your child's reaction to situations and various parenting techniques. This knowledge will enable you to anticipate his behavior so that you can adjust your parenting plan accordingly.

Respond to Your Child's Temperament

Temperament is relatively stable from birth. These traits are neither good nor bad. They are just your child's (and your) approach to life. You will be more successful if you select parenting techniques that work with your child's temperament rather than ones that oppose it. While most techniques work with various temperaments, some work better with one temperament than another. If your child generally falls under the "difficult" category, you will need to pay close attention to the more controlling techniques presented along Paths 6 through 8.

Activity level (general physical activity)

Your active child requires you to be consistent and firm. His behavior can quickly get out of control. You will need to use all of the preventive approaches that are described along Paths 5 and 6 as well as the more controlling parenting techniques found on Paths 7 and 8. Your active child's environment, especially his room, should be calming and void of stimulation, while your quiet child's room should be decorated with toys and items that entice interaction (see Path 5, "Set the stage"). The computer, which holds the attention of the active child and stimulates the quiet child, can, when used judicially, be used to teach new skills to your child.

Regularity (predictability of biological factors)

Having a schedule is comforting to the regular child and will help the irregular child anticipate, and thus adjust to, the schedule. For your non-reader you can create a schedule using pictures. If both you and your child have low regularity, your family schedule may be very flexible with people eating when they are hungry rather than at a scheduled time. Your schedule may vary greatly depending on the day of the week. If family members have different needs for regularity, you will need to negotiate a solution.

Distractibility (reaction to the task)

The discussion under activity level also applies here. You will need to provide your easily distracted child a space void of visual and auditory distractions. If possible, prepare a cubby-like space for your distractible child to do his homework. In contrast, your child with low distractibility will be successful doing homework at the kitchen table where you can help him as you prepare a meal. Whenever your child has homework or another task that must be completed, put him in an environment where he can succeed.

Sensory threshold (reaction to sensory stimuli)

Music or white noise increases the focus of some children by reducing their need to seek other stimuli; other children need total quiet. Don't assume that your child's reaction to silence or background noise is the

48

same as yours. Experiment with various types of background noise and total silence to determine what works best for your child. Move important tasks, such as homework, to an area where the sensory background meets your child's sensory threshold needs.   *OK most place*

Approach/withdrawal (initial response to situations or strangers)

You must teach your child how to respond to strangers. This may be challenging if your child has strong approach tendencies. You don't want to scare your child but you will need to teach her whom to approach and when. If your baby or young child is shy, you need to teach family members and friends how to approach your child in a calming way. Ask them to sit quietly, hold a favorite toy, and wait for her to approach. Once she approaches, the adult must move slowly and quietly, focusing on the toy rather than the child. Only after numerous approaches by the child should the adult look at her. Be sure to smile with a closed mouth, as teeth may scare the child.

As the shy child grows and enters school, she may not be willing to ask a teacher for help. Role-play asking for help. Discuss the situation with the teacher. Don't expect to teach your child to be an extrovert, but you can modify her behavior to a point that makes her life easier.

Adaptability (length of time needed to change)

Be patient and support your child as he adjusts to a new classroom, new school, home, or neighborhood. Pay particular attention to the discussion on working with the school on Path 10, "Be a double advocate."

Persistence (unwillingness to give up, stubbornness)

You may be proud of your persistent child as she works on a project or as she develops her athletic or musical skill but become totally exasperated when she confronts your rules. The more persistent your child, the more important it is for you to be consistent and to teach your rules. The reasons for your decisions need to be discussed at a developmentally appropriate level with your child but not when you are having a conflict. Leave those discussions for nonconfrontational times.

Mood (prevailing emotional state)

If your child frequently approaches life in a negative, cranky, and unhappy manner, teach him that it pays to be positive. Ignore his negative behaviors and pay attention to him when he is in a more positive frame of mind. Discuss the happy things that occur in your family. Your child is smart and will quickly learn what actions get your attention (his happy face or his sad face) and will increase the behaviors that get your attention. If your child's temperament is pervasively sad, you are not going to change him into a happy-go-lucky child, but you can provide an opportunity to learn the advantages of being positive.

Of course, never ignore signs of depression, such as threats to inflict self-injury or the failure to receive pleasure from situations that usually bring him happiness. Depression is a medical problem and dangerous at any age. Do not ignore it! If the prevailing sadness is not modified by your paying attention to the happy times, if it gets worse, or if it occurs in a previously happy child, you must take your child for professional evaluation, as depression often leads to disinterest in school, difficulty making friends, and low self-esteem. It can also lead to suicide, especially as the child gets older. Too much is at stake to ignore depression.

Intensity (strength of the child's response) 1/8

The defiant, willful child will benefit from parenting techniques that reduce confrontations, minimize verbal interaction, and require a

reduce confrontation

clearly defined response from the child. Pay close attention to Paths 7 and 8, which describe appropriate responses to inappropriate behaviors.

How does your temperament interact with your child's? Are there modifications you need to make in your temperament? Temperament, like all inborn characteristics, is resistant to change, but it can be modified. Consider what alterations you and your child can make that will work for both of you.

Discover Your Child's Interests and Abilities

Your child has unique interests and abilities that will bring new richness to your family. His interests are what he enjoys and chooses to do. His ability is the speed with which he acquires a new skill or knowledge as well as the level of expertise achieved. If success is achieved easily in a given area, your child may become more interested in that activity. Likewise, an interest in an area may spur effort that leads to high achievement.

Give your child time and opportunities to experience different activities. If he uses his free time primarily to watch television or play computer games, he will have limited exposure to the vast array of opportunities provided in our society. Limit the time available for technological activities and provide resources (i.e., balls, a musical instrument, records, art supplies, books, and trips) that will introduce him to possible new interests. Introduce him to your interests as well. Include him in your daily bike ride. Take nature walks with him. Expand his world and watch how he responds.

There are things you can do to determine your child's level of interest (or disinterest) in a specific activity. Observe:

- Whether he chooses to do it during his free time;
- How long or frequently he engages in the activity;
- Whether he is disappointed or relieved when a scheduled activity is cancelled;
- Whether the activity acts as a reinforcer.

You can learn a great deal about your child's interest in an activity by watching her response to having a day off. Does she seem relieved (low or no interest), or does she request to do it on her own (high interest)?

You can also determine your child's interest in an activity by observing whether it acts as a reinforcer. For example, if your child is on a basketball team and you tell him that he can shoot baskets as soon as he completes his chores, does he hurry to complete the chores so he can play basketball? If so, basketball is acting as a reinforcer, and he has a high interest in the sport. If, however, the prospect of shooting baskets does not encourage him to quickly complete his other tasks, his interest is minimal.

Some children prefer diversity, while others will show a strong preference for one type of activity. There is no right or wrong choice, just your child's choice. If you try to live through your child by pushing him to achieve in the areas where you either excelled or wished you had excelled, you are setting yourself and your child up for failure. Get to know your child. If you share interests, great! If his interests are different from yours, support his interests and enjoy them; they will expand your world.

If your child is forced into a program that is of mild interest or no interest to him, you will create friction and make parenting hard. It's not worth it! If you demean his area of interest, he will view it as personally demeaning. If you prevent him from pursuing his interest, you are teaching him not to set goals and pursue them. Setting and pursuing goals are paramount for becoming a motivated person.

Consider the Unique Needs of Your Special-Needs Child

If you have a special-needs child, remember that he is first and foremost a child. Like all children, he needs you to use parenting techniques that will control his inappropriate behaviors and will teach him socially appropriate ones. No pill will do this. No medicine will teach him how to become a productive member of society. *Only you can do that.*

Therefore, like all parents, you need to identify your child's temperament and level of development so you can create a parenting plan unique to your child. When your child was diagnosed with a special need, you were probably given a list of behaviors to expect. Your child may exhibit all or only some of them. Look at your *child* as an individual. Rather than focusing on your child's special education label, look at your child's behaviors and compare them to the descriptions of the various temperaments described earlier. If one of the behaviors associated with his special needs is hyperactivity, select parenting techniques suitable for a highly active child. If your child's special need includes violent responses to intervention, you are dealing with an intensity problem and will need to use techniques that focus on calming your child.

While the unique aspects of parenting a child with special needs are beyond the scope of this book, it does contain important information for parents of special-needs children. Your parenting plan will include both techniques you have been given based on child's diagnosis and the techniques explained in this book.

Consider the Unique Needs of Your Adopted Child

Our three adopted children, who share no genetics, each responded to being adopted in their own unique way. They enabled me to observe how an understanding of adoption develops and changes over time. They taught me that adoption can create unique situations.

SCENARIO

"My, where did you get those brown eyes?" Mark, a thirty-something, asked three-year-old Timmy. Mark looked at the other four family members and said, "Everyone else in your family has blue eyes."

Timmy covered his eyes and looked down.

"His eyes are so beautiful—that's why you notice them," Mom told Mark. "If you had looked more carefully at the rest of our eyes, you would have observed that each of us has different eyes."

Even after being assured that each family member had eyes perfect for him or her and that all people are both alike and different, for several weeks Timmy hid his eyes from strangers. A child wants to be like his family, but when a child is adopted and shares no genetics with his siblings or parents, people will notice differences. If you and your child come from different ethnic groups, the differences in appearance will be very noticeable. Your comfort or discomfort with the variation in your family will influence your child's acceptance or lack thereof. When your child is learning to talk, refer to yourself as "mama" or "dada." If someone asks, "Do you know her real mother?" say, "Yes, I'm her real mother. We were not told the name of the birth mother." How wonderful that the adopted child has her real parents close by each and every day.

Bonding, which leads to attachment, is essential for your child's development. If you adopt an infant, the attachment process will occur in the same manner as it would have occurred if you had birthed the infant. But if you are one of the many parents adopting older children from this country or abroad, you will need to deliberately take steps to create a bond. Carve out two or more weeks for just you and your child. Grandparents and friends will just have to wait. If there are a lot of people in and out, then your home will be too much like her previous situation. People came and went, and finally they all left. She needs stability and the assurance that you will always be there to provide love and to meet all her needs. Seeking out a parent when she needs help is one indicator that a bond may be developing. If you have any doubts about the development of attachment, seek professional help.

The child adopted before he was old enough to remember his biological mother will need to have the adoption process explained at a level he can understand. The child's understanding of adoption is determined by his cognitive development. An infant learns by associating sensory experiences. For example, the child learns the word "ball" through hearing the word while having the sensory experience of playing with the ball. Likewise, when your baby or toddler hears the word "adoption" while experiencing your love, he will associate the word "adoption" with comfort and love.

Preschool children assume everything is like they see it and, therefore, assume all families are created in the same way. Preschool children cannot comprehend that a big adult could lack the resources needed to care for a child. While her preschool understanding of the adoption process is limited, she can learn that it includes being a part of a loving family.

During the early elementary school years, the child starts to understand that there are multiple ways of viewing things. This enables your child, adopted as an infant, to understand, for the first time, that families are formed in different ways. He can understand the basics of conception and that he has birth parents. For the first time, he realizes that before his mom and dad chose him, someone had to give him away. This new understanding can brings forth new feelings, which may include abandonment, anger, and fear of being parentless. If your child feels a sense of abandonment, he may conclude that he must have done something terrible to cause the biological parent to reject him. Telling him you love him and that you explicitly chose him does not diminish the feeling of abandonment. He has experienced a sorrow akin to the death of a parent. He needs a time to mourn and to forgive. Forgiveness is not what we do for the other person; it is what we do for ourselves. When your child forgives her biological parent and accepts that there were social pressures—unrelated to who she is—that caused the biological parent to seek an adoptive home for her, then she can begin to heal. As a Christian, I use God's forgiveness of our sins as a basis for discussing forgiveness. Discussing the social climate that probably led to her being placed up for adoption can also help her understand that the biological parents were acting out of love for her.

Your adopted child may fear that he could have remained parentless his entire life. Television news stories about children in need of adoption or children in foster homes can rekindle the fear of being parentless. Keep in mind that even children who live with their biological parent(s) have fears related to becoming parentless. Your child needs to know there is a "safety net" and what it is.

It is imperative to remember that the fears and concerns we have discussed are not a reflection on your parenting or your child's love for you, the adoptive parent, but the outgrowth of normal human fears and an awareness of the social environment in which we live.

A child who remembers the birth mother may want to contact her. Work with your social worker to determine what is best for your child. Children adopted from other countries benefit from maintaining contacts with other children and adults from their former country as a way of experiencing their cultural heritage. Open adoptions have increased in recent years. Your child's contact with the birth parents will be guided by the legal agreement made at the time of the adoption. As a young adult, our daughter found her biological mother. This has been a very positive experience for everyone involved.

Regardless of the age of your child at adoption and regardless of whether your child does or does not have contact with the biological parent, it is important to present the biological parent in a positive light. Your child knows that he carries the genes of his biological parents and therefore will attach your description of the biological parent to himself. If you say the parent was "no good," the child will conclude that deep down he is "no good."

At a workshop for people preparing to adopt, one young man asked, "But what do you say if you know the child was taken away because of drug abuse or crime?" I told him to teach understanding, empathy, and forgiveness. Explain that some people are raised in environments in which they are not provided help, and getting help makes a difference. Assure your child that you are there to help. Let your child know that genes don't determine who you become. They're a part of how you need to approach life in order to reach your goals, but they don't decide your goals. Remind your child that she is unique and that her home and opportunities make her a different person. She can set and achieve goals.

Throughout his life, your child will be confronted with the importance of genetics. Every time he goes to a new doctor, he will be asked about his family's health history; therefore, if you have any contact with the parent, seek health information to learn whether he should use special precautions to avoid future health problems. The biological parents, present or not, are undeniably a part of your child. I firmly believe that reuniting a biological parent with her biological child can be very positive. The biological parent cannot go back in time and be the one who comforted the crying child or cheered her on to success. I am grateful that she gave life to my child and will always remember her in my prayers. Encourage your child to celebrate her genetic gifts. Don't harp on the word adoption. Don't ignore it, either. Just embrace it.

Path 4

Expect Age-Typical Behavior

Your child is both unique and like other children. On the preceding path we explored the uniqueness of your child. On this path we will explore the similarities between your child and other children her age.

As your child grows, her behaviors change, and so must your parenting. Your child's level of development determines how she will react to various parenting techniques. Keep this section handy so you can adjust your parenting as your child matures.

Respond to Developmental Changes

Recognize age-typical behavior

A complete study of child development is beyond the scope of this book. I will limit my comments to behaviors that are crucial to the parenting process. While your child's skills will emerge in a predictable sequence, I will not attach specific ages to any behavior or skill, because your child will develop them on her personal time schedule. Providing the sequence of skill development allows me to explain how to both support your child's present level of development and prepare your child for the next level of development. But, if you want to know the age certain behaviors frequently appear, you can get this information by going online to get a developmental chart. They can be helpful or lead you astray, depending on what information they provide. Charts can provide:

- *A range of ages* when most children develop a skill;
- *The average age* at which children develop a skill;

- *The critical age* by which children should have developed a skill before medical advice is sought.

Determine what type of developmental chart you are using. A developmental chart that gives a range of ages, such as the Denver Developmental Chart, indicates the ages when 25, 50, and 75 percent of children develop that specific skill. This chart can help you see where your child's development falls but cannot identify giftedness or developmental delays. Most of the charts online provide lists of behaviors that develop over a specified time, such as one month for infants and six months to a year for older children. They provide general information that is fun to know but is only minimally helpful.

The most misleading chart is the one that gives just one age—the average age—when various skills develop. Keep in mind that, when the median is used, half of all children develop the skills before the listed age and half of all children develop it after that age. Are half of all children gifted or slow? No way! Never use a developmental chart to determine whether your child is gifted or slow.

If you are concerned about your child's development and wonder whether you need to seek professional help, you may want to select a developmental chart that provides the *critical age*, that is, the age at which 90 percent of all children have developed that particular skill. Your pediatrician or a specialist will then do a screening test to determine whether your child needs intervention—which is most effective when given early.

As your child grows, so will your ability to interpret his behavior. This skill begins early as you notice that your newborn is either calm or crying with his whole body. Initially your baby can only communicate comfort or discomfort, but as your baby develops, his cries become varied, and you learn to distinguish between cries that indicate pain and those that indicate exhaustion. This ability to interpret why your child is crying is extremely valuable as it enables you to select your response based, not on crying, but on his need. You were not born with this skill; you develop it through astute, ongoing observations of your child.

Support emerging skills

To learn a new skill your child, regardless of his age, must be developmentally ready. He must have the:

- *Prior skills* needed to perform the new skill;
- *Physical and/or mental structure* needed to learn the new skill.

Your child's physical development proceeds from the head down, therefore your baby holds his head up before he sits up, and he sits before he walks. Since walking requires holding up the head, keeping the back straight, and having strong legs your baby cannot learn to walk until all those physical structures have developed. Trying to teach a four-month-old to walk is not only futile, but also injurious to the undeveloped bones in his legs. The bones and the muscles in the back and the legs must be ready to hold up the child.

Your job is to provide environmental supports for the emerging skills. For example, when she is working on holding up her head, cup your hand under her head to support it. Keep it there when she attempts to lift her head so she will have a place to rest her head. When her back has gained strength, provide both opportunity to sit and the support needed to avoid straining her back. When her legs become stronger, provide low tables that she can pull up on and walk around. Never try to force your child to develop a specific physical skill. Your goal must always be to support the skills that are emerging.

While your child's biological, inborn timetable creates the window when a skill can develop, his ultimate success will be determined by his *individual characteristics* and *environment*. For example, individual characteristics, such as temperament, play a role in when the baby will learn to walk. A baby who is adventuresome is going to learn to walk more quickly than a fearful child who dislikes falling. Your child also needs an environment that promotes "practice walking." A child needs a place to move, furniture to pull up on and walk around, and an adult who holds his hand and claps when he bravely lets go.

Walk from Birth to Age Two: Sensory Exploration Propels Development

Development proceeds rapidly as your baby goes from an infant who stays put to a toddler on the run. She explores her new world with all her senses—taste, smell, touch, sight, and hearing.

Promote bonding and attachment

Remember how you felt when you held your baby for the first time? It was an emotional rush unlike any other. When my daughter called to tell me I had a grandson, she said, "Oh, Mother. I have never felt such a surge of love as when I first held Alex." I assured her that I, too, was astonished at the emotions that welled within me when I first held my baby. A psychologist friend commented, "Having a baby turns your brain to mush! My feelings and behaviors are beyond rational." Two fathers, who were serving on a panel for future adoptive parents, described the intense emotions that welled within them when they held their babies for the first time.

Your emotional outpouring, which is the first step toward bonding, and your baby's sensory experiences are very important in the attachment process. The baby sees your face, smells your body, feels your touch, and hears your voice as her needs are met. Because you keep reappearing and meeting her needs, trust begins. This trust leads to bonding, which over time, becomes attachment.

Attachment creates the foundation necessary for your child to express and experience love. If attachment fails to develop, a baby will not develop physically, socially, or emotionally. She will attain developmental milestones later than her peers. As an adult she will have difficulty developing an emotional connection with another person.

If you or someone you know suffers from postpartum depression or is having problems bonding with her baby, urge her to seek professional help. Medical help may be needed to help her enjoy and bond with her baby.

If you are adopting, ask if the child had a significant person during his first two years of life. Once a baby has attached to one person, he will be able to attach to another person. If there was no opportunity to attach to a significant person in his life, ask about the baby's prognosis for being able to attach and how you can foster it. Attachment is the beginning of your child's positive social and emotional development. Therefore, if it is not occurring, seek professional help.

Encourage your "budding scientist"

When you see your baby pick up an object, you know where it is going—into her mouth. As a budding scientist, your baby uses the senses of seeing, touching, tasting, feeling, and hearing to learn about her environment. In fact, your baby's prenatal hearing softens her transition into the world. Before birth, your baby becomes accustomed to the noise level of your home, to your choice of music, to your television programs, and to your voice. In the midst of the newness of birth, your baby hears something familiar—the sounds of her home and your voice. After birth, your baby's development is propelled by the use of her *senses* and her *movements* to investigate her world. Sensation and movement are instrumental in the development of *attachment* (discussed previously), the development of *concepts and knowledge* about the world, and the discovery that she can cause things to happen. Prepare for your budding scientist's exploration by creating a safe place for exploration.

Your newborn experiences can help him create knowledge and distinguish one item from another. For example, the infant sucks on his mother's breast or a bottle's nipple and concludes that it is soft and makes his tummy feel good. He sucks on a pacifier and discovers that some things that he sucks on are soft but do nothing for his tummy. He associates the visual stimuli with those two experiences and soon shows he knows the difference between the breast or bottle and a pacifier. You did not teach him this concept. He learned it, as he learns all his knowledge, from his daily sensory experiences.

Not only will your baby's ability to associate and integrate sensory experiences lead to emotional bonding with you and to her knowledge about her immediate world, it will enable her to distinguish and recognize the other people in her environment, including grandparents, caretakers, and friends. Since she has associated the various sensory factors that represent you, she will recognize your voice and be calmed when you call from the other room. You want your child, as she expands her horizons, to mentally take you with her wherever she goes. This is the beginning of your values, your rules, and your expectations staying with her even when you are not visibly present.

Your baby's increasing mobility expands his available sensory experiences and thus his opportunities to learn new concepts. For example, he learns about a table by crawling under it, patting the tabletop, biting the edge, and sitting on it. These experiences that enabled him to have a concept of "table" eventually makes the word "table" meaningful. Concept development is paramount for language development and must precede it. Therefore, it is important that you provide your baby safe places where he can learn concepts through movement and sensory exploration.

When you have to stop your infant from playing with something, use distraction, because out of sight (and the other senses) is out of mind. Pick your baby up and move her to another area and give her something to manipulate. Even after your child develops an understanding that objects still exist even if she cannot see them, the sensory awareness of the replacement object is so great she can easily be distracted and encouraged to play with the object placed before her. If a parent uses an angry voice and says "no" the baby will associate the anger with the face saying it. Do you want your baby to associate anger or love with you? It is so easy to smile at your baby as you distract her.

As his mobility increases, so will his learning. His little brain is moving just as fast, or faster, than his legs and arms. Your little scientist is developing his mind as he uses these rapidly emerging physical abilities. Indeed, since development proceeds from the head down, the first part of your child's body to reach adult size is the head and the brain.

Not only does your baby learn concepts through her senses and her movements, she also learns that she can cause things to happen. First she learns that she can choose to grasp and let go of an object. As a newborn, her grasp of your finger, which is so strong that you could lift her a few inches off of her bed, was a reflex action. The reflex grasp is eventually replaced with a deliberate one. This act leads to a deliberate reaching for an object, such as a rattle. Since her arms frequently move involuntarily, the rattle makes a sound. She integrates the sensory experiences of seeing the rattle, feeling the muscle movement in the arm, and hearing the sounds made by the rattle. After numerous experiences of these three together, she will deliberately move her arm to cause the sound. She has discovered that she can cause something to happen. This early understanding is the foundation for motivation. People who believe they can cause things to happen are more likely to set goals and work to achieve them.

Your baby is carefully storing months of accidental sensory experiences. She accidentally knocks her spoon off her tray. Mom picks it up. She accidentally knocks it off again, and Mom picks it up again. She remembers these accidental drops and begins to realize she can drop the spoon at will. Thus, she starts to drop it intentionally. Being a budding scientist, she wonders, "If I drop the spoon, will Mom pick it up?" Mom does! Your baby is delighted, and you should be too. For the first time, your baby's actions are planned and executed in order to get a result. For the first time, you are faced with selecting a response to purposeful behavior.

You can choose from several responses—playing pick-up, distraction, planned ignoring, or confrontation. I will describe each approach and then discuss what I call side effects of that approach. Side effects are the unintentional, long-term outcome of the chosen method of parenting. I want you to start thinking of parenting approaches both in the context of how they fit your immediate need and your long-term parenting goals, not only in this situation but all future discussions of responses to your child's behavior.

I frequently chose to play pick-up as I enjoyed my baby's new skill and wanted her to realize she could cause something to happen. Your parenting goals, available time, and your temperament will influence how long you play pick-up. The side effect of this approach is building a positive relationship that will serve you now and later.

You can select distraction. When time does not permit game-playing, this nonconfrontational approach is an excellent choice. Talk to your baby as this will cause him to focus on your face. Play "airplane"— that is, let the spoon "fly" the food to your child's mouth as you gently hold his hands. Distraction, which lets you have a calm day and allows you to redirect your baby's behavior, is a fast path to cooperation. This approach requires you to be calm and works well with most babies. Like the previous approach, the side effect of this approach is building a positive relationship.

The third approach, planned ignoring (see Path 8, "Ignore attention-getting behaviors"), requires the parent to ignore the dropped spoon. Planned ignoring may initially bring on a screaming child, especially if your child ranks high in persistence and/or intensity. This will require all items within the reach of the baby to be removed. Determine whether your baby will be safer in the chair or on the floor. Once your baby can no longer reach the food and is in a safe location, ignore his screaming and kicking. This approach also requires you, as the parent, to remain calm when the baby is not. When the crying stops, calmly pick up the spoon and help the baby feed himself. Stop feeding if the screaming or kicking returns and repeat the procedure discussed previously. Planned ignoring provides excellent long-term results and is highly effective when you decide to end this game. Its side effect is to establish you as the person in control without creating negative interpersonal conflicts.

If you use the common, angry response of "no," you are inviting a confrontation, and your baby will, most likely, accept your challenge. Confrontation, which will leave both you and your child mad and upset, is a lose-lose proposition. The side effect you have created will affect your child's response to you now and in the future; you are starting a *negative pattern* of interaction with your child.

Each of these approaches has a positive or negative side effect that will impact your long-term relationship. You can't control the side effect produced by a given approach, but you can select an approach that gives you the long-range results you want. As your child matures, dropping spoons will no longer interest her, and she will replace it with new behaviors that will challenge your parenting skills.

Provide for safe exploration

Your baby will develop into a toddler who can move faster than you can. The need for safe places to explore has increased, and you will need to go through your entire home to make certain you are making your home safe. Remove items that may injure your child or be broken if manipulated or examined. Put childproof locks on cabinets and doors. Put medicine and cleaning supplies up. Get a list of dangerous items from your pediatrician, and make your home safe for exploration. Exploration is vital for your toddler's development and learning; therefore, you need to provide a safe place and safe items for manipulation and sensory exploration.

One of the myths of parenting is that parents should leave the items in their home as they were before they had a child and just teach the child to leave them alone. This creates a dangerous environment and one that promotes confrontations. You will find yourself saying, "No!" over and over. Your child will eventually copy you and soon use "No!" over and over with you. There probably *will* be items that you cannot remove, and you can teach your child not to play with those few items, but remove what you can.

Rather than attempt to stop the exploration altogether, redirect it. Sensory and physical exploration is vital for concept development. Concepts are vital for language development. Language development is vital for communication, and communication is vital to all areas of parenting.

Use age-appropriate communication

Your parenting will be easier if your child uses words to tell you why he is angry rather than using hitting and kicking to communicate unhappiness. The language your child needs to communicate his needs and to understand the expectations of others begins in infancy and continues throughout his life.

Your infant's first mode of communication is crying. One of the detrimental myths of parenting is that picking up a crying infant will spoil him. Crying is the infant's only means of communicating hunger or discomfort. If you are perceptive of your newborn's needs and meet them quickly, you will have a calm infant that uses crying only to signal a need. Numerous studies have found that babies that are purposefully left to cry, as a means of preventing "spoiling," are still fussy after being fed and diapered, whereas babies whose parents respond quickly to the *needs* expressed by the cries are much calmer after being fed and diapered. Your newborn is incapable of plotting to control you. He just responds to his sensory experiences.

Will your child try to manipulate you? Of course, but not during these early months. Earlier I discussed how your baby goes from accidentally dropping a spoon to *purposefully* dropping it as a way to initiate the game of pick-up. This signals a new level of thinking, namely, "I can cause things to happen." At this point, your child may try various approaches, including crying, to manipulate you. When that happens, your parenting techniques need to change.

You need to replace crying as a way of communicating with using *words to communicate.* Linguists have determined that children throughout the world go through the following sequence when developing language:

1. Babbling, making the sounds of all the languages.
2. Echolalia babbling, is making the sounds he hears.
3. Word formation, first, a single-word utterances: next, two-word utterances. Utterances gradually increase in length.
4. Parts of speech appear in the following order:
   a. Words that name people or objects (such as "ball").
   b. Action words (such as "up" and "bounce").
   c. Descriptive words (such as "red").

Creating speech sounds requires fine-motor skills, which develop in a predictable sequence. Making the "m" sound requires only your lips. In contrast, making the American "r" sound requires both sides of your tongue to curl up. The fine motor control needed to make a specific sound must develop before your child can make that sound. Therefore, your child's speech sounds will emerge in a predictable sequence.

Your child's ability to *understand* the spoken language precedes his ability to use speech to demonstrate those understandings and is greatly affected by his environment. There are many things you can do to support his developing language concepts:

- Name the object the child is holding or looking at, such as mama or shoe. This parallel talking—i.e., using the word that names or describes what the child is holding or doing—will connect words to concepts.
- Read and talk to your child.
- Provide an environment safe for movement and exploration to enable him to develop concepts.
- Give your child simple directions, such as, "put the book on the shelf." This will teach him relationship words, increase his memory, and promote following directions.

It is important to say words one at a time. Have you ever listened to a foreign language and wondered where one word ended and the next one began? Your baby needs to hear words in isolation.

By introducing the parts of speech in the order they appear normally—that is, nouns first followed by verbs and then eventually adjectives—you are presenting new words when the child is most ready to learn them. To promote spoken language, *recognize and accept* the present level of language development and then *model the next level* by speaking it back to the child.

Present Language Skill	Accept It	Model Next Level
1. Naming object, such as ball	"Ba, yes, ba."	Ball
2. Add verb to the noun	Ball	Ball bounce (or ball roll)
3. Add adjective to the noun	Ball bounce (or ball woll)	Blue ball bounce

Teach "ball" before adding "bounce" or "roll." Teach "ball bounce" before teaching "red" or "blue ball bounces." The baby will find it easier to learn if the name of the object is taught before the adjective used to describe it. Remember to keep your interaction fun.

Should you also talk to your baby in complete sentences? Absolutely! Your baby needs to learn the cadence (rhythm) of his language. Your child needs to learn how to end a string of sounds with an inflection that indicates an exclamation, a question, or a statement. You may have noticed that your baby's babbling frequently ends with an inflection that makes it sound like a sentence or question.

Make language useful! Once the child has the fine-motor skill necessary to create the sounds, don't accept the grunt-and-point approach to communicating. For example, if a child is capable of saying wa-wa or an approximation of that sound, don't accept a grunt-and-point request for water. Require wa-wa or another developmentally appropriate vocalization.

By the time your child is two, he is bombarding you with language, and you may wish for just a moment of silence. Hang in there. Words are your ally in developing appropriate behavior.

Know when "no" doesn't mean "no"

When you use "no," you are *modeling* the word and how to use it. Just as you modeled words like "water" to teach your child, every time you said "no," you were modeling how to use that word to control others. You can't pick the times you want modeling to work and turn your child's mind off at other times. Modeling always works.

You use words to control your child. You told your two-year-old, "Bring me the ball," and he did. When he hit you, you said, "No." He didn't want to stop, but you made him. Now comes the big question in his two-year-old mind: will words work for me like they do for Mom? Can I, by saying 'no,' make Mom stop?" Your two-year-old is developing a sense of self by exploring his ability to control himself and others. As he explores how "no" works for him, you will get ten to a hundred "no's" back for every "no" you used with him.

Don't take his "no" seriously. If you are putting on his coat and he says "no," ignore it and distract him with talk about where you are going. This teaches your child that "no" does not control you.

If you take "no" as a personal affront and say something like, "Don't you tell me no!," you have just thrown down the gauntlet and invited your child to a head-to-head fight. Of course you are bigger. Of course you have the power. You will "win," *but* your two-year-old is asking himself, "What has my 'no' done? It made Mom mad, just like her 'no' made me mad. 'No' works!"

I have seen parents try to find alternative ways of saying "no," such as "don't do that." That doesn't change the nature of the interaction. Rather than using the negative, tell your toddler what behavior you expect, such as, "Put your arm in the sleeve." "No" is just a little two-letter word and not a four-letter word to be avoided at all cost. "No" is sometimes the most sensible word to use (see Path 7, "Know when to say "no"). In fact, you are going to want your child to learn when to say "no" to his peers.

During these first two and a half to three years of your child's life, you have laid the foundation for your interactions with him. He has grown and changed. Be prepared. There are big changes ahead and your parenting skills need to keep up with these changes.

Walk through the Preschool Years: The "Eyes" Have It

Let's explore the thinking of your preschool child and how this determines behavior and reactions to your parenting techniques. Psychologists have studied thought patterns by trying the same tasks with preschool children of different cultures and generations and observing their answers. I have described some of those tasks so you can use them to explore the thinking of your preschool child.

Expect decisions to be based on how things look

Your child's level of development determines how he thinks. Your preschool child cannot mentally manipulate what he sees and therefore concludes that things are exactly as they look at the moment. For fun, you might try this with your three- or four-year-old (or a young five-year-old). Find two glasses (or two measuring cups) the same size and have your child tell you when you have poured the same amount of juice in each of them. Ask him again if both the glasses have the same amount of juice. Then have him pour the juice from one of the glasses into a wide glass that can hold a cup and a half of liquid and the other glass of juice into a tall, skinny glass that holds just one cup of liquid. Ask him if the two glasses have the same amount of juice. If he says no, ask him which glass of juice has more. He will probably select the tall, skinny glass. Ask him why. He will say the juice is at the top, or he'll point to the two levels of juice. Even though he poured an equal amount of juice into each glass himself, he will pick the tall, skinny glass, because the liquid line is higher—it *looks* like more. He does not consider how it looked before he poured it.

You can use this thinking to avoid conflict. For example, when my youngest was determined to have as much to drink as her older brothers, I kept her happy by giving her a skinny glass and her brothers wider glasses. Since she could see that each glass was full to the top, she was content.

Expect your child to consider only one factor at a time

During this stage your child will consider only one factor at a time and will disregard other relevant factors. In the preceding example, the preschooler did not consider both the height and the width of the glasses—only whether the juice came to the top of the glass.

Another fun thing to try with your preschooler requires twenty pennies. Have your child make two lines of ten pennies. Place the second line of pennies above the first line. Have her arrange them so she is convinced that the two rows of pennies have the same number of pennies (see Path 10, "one-to-one correspondence"). Leave one line of pennies untouched, but spread the other row of pennies so there is space between each penny. Moving your finger the length of each row of pennies, ask if this row of pennies has the *same number* of pennies as this other row. Always ask if they are the same number as this suggests to her that they are equal. She will say "no." Next ask which has more pennies. She will pick the spread-out row of pennies. Ask her how she knows it has more.

Return the pennies to their original position. Keep ten pennies in each group, but try various ways of spacing them. Each time ask if they are the *same number* of pennies. If not, which is more and why is it more. Listen to the reason she gives for her choice. In this example (as well as the one where she poured the liquid), she does not consider the change process, only the final position. Because of this, she will not yet be able to understand addition and subtraction in math (see Path 10, "Countdown to success").

Expect your child to ignore the change process

In the preceding examples, the preschooler did not consider the change process. She focused on how it looked at the end. This way of thinking makes moving objects very dangerous. For example, your preschooler does not consider that the swing will return to where it was a second ago. He sees the swing at the back, makes a judgment call based on how it looks at the moment, and concludes that now he can run past it. Of course, the swing returns, and he gets knocked down. Even if you point out the swing's location when it is high and how it returns to its starting place, he will continue to make his decision based on how it looks at the moment. Rather than expecting your preschooler to consider the change process—that is, the swing will return—teach him to walk along a designated path around the swing. Preschool children regard rules as absolute and can therefore be taught to follow one consistently, but—just like anything else—it will need to be taught over and over to "stick." Since children forget rules, you may decide to install a protective barrier around your child's swing or decide not to have a swing. You still need to teach the rule, as your child will encounter swings at playgrounds and/or preschool. He needs to be taught and retaught the rule that he must stay a long, long way away from the swing.

His failure to consider the change process also makes streets dangerous. Rather than relying on his understanding that the car's location will change, teach the rule that only adults can go into the street to get balls or other items. Don't expect him to understand the reasons for the rule. Later, when your child is in elementary school, his thinking will expand; he will be able to understand that the swing will return and the car will move to where his ball rolled. During the preschool years, protect your child by teaching safety rules. Also remember that all people forget things, especially when they are excited. This will help you anticipate when a reminder is needed or supervision is required.

Artwork by Aundrea

Expect limited understanding of what causes things to happen

Your preschool child believes that events that occur together have a causal relationship. Your preschool child may be stacking blocks when they suddenly fall down. He may accuse a sibling or playmate of knocking down his blocks just because the other child was playing in the area when the blocks fell. He knows he didn't knock them down, so he concludes that the other child must have caused them to fall. When one child blames another child for a mishap, calmly gather information before jumping to a conclusion. The other child may, or may not, have knocked them down.

On one occasion, when I was observing my student teacher in a preschool setting, I was sitting just beyond the rug where the children were playing with their blocks. My student was sitting on the floor near a child that was stacking blocks. The blocks fell. The child whimpered, pointed to me, and said, "She knocked them down." My student looked at me, and her face fell. I felt so sorry for my student. She wisely discussed what makes blocks fall. The child was using preschool reasoning—the blocks fell for an unknown reason, and I was the unknown in the room.

Whether your child is the one doing the accusing or the one being accused, remember that the preschooler is not "lying" as an adult defines lying—that is, saying what is known to be untrue. He may truly think his friend knocked them down or, as in the previously discussed situation, that the unknown person must have caused the event. Ask your child to show you several things that could cause something to happen; in this situation, ask him to show you various things that could make the blocks fall. These are things he can see and therefore understand. Seeing multiple possibilities sets the stage for the next level of thinking. When your child is approaching the elementary years, you can "challenge" his preschool way of thinking by modeling how to consider intent. This sets the stage for an extended understanding of what actually causes things to happen.

Expect your child to consider only his or her view

Since preschool thinking relies on absolutes, a preschooler concludes that others see things like she does. Just as she cannot do the mental task of considering both the height and width of a glass, the child cannot consider two views, that is, her view and a friend's view. When my son, who loved rolling down the hill, was unable to convince the petite neighbor girl to give it a try, he pushed her down the hill. He was certain she would love it. She didn't. Fortunately the other mother, who was also standing there, was not upset. My son promised not to do it again. I immediately established the rule that you cannot push someone down a hill. They played peacefully and happily the rest of the day and many times in the future.

When preschool thinking results in social problems, you should correct the behavior calmly and use it as a teaching time. Challenging your child's way of thinking has minimal impact until she is almost ready to move to the next level of development. Let your understanding of preschool-thinking keep you from overreacting to your child's (or another's) inappropriate behavior. The most effective way of getting the desired behavior is to calmly tell her the behavior you want in this situation.

Since your preschooler believes everyone thinks and feels like she does, she will show great empathy for you or another child who is sick or hurt. She knows how that feels and understands that you feel the same. That makes the preschool years the ideal time to teach empathy! However, if you and your preschool child have different feelings about something, she won't understand. That will change as she matures. She will start to consider multiple factors as she enters the elementary school years.

Teach what you consider to be good or bad

Your preschool child's definition of "good" and "bad" is very simple: what gets him in trouble is "bad," and what is praised or at least allowed is "good." Your child will learn what you regard as "good" behaviors by observing which behaviors work. If temper tantrums, whining, and crying are behaviors that work, your child will decide that those behaviors are both useful and "good." Therefore, it is important that the behaviors you want are the only ones that work for your child.

"Mine! I want it *now!*" Sound familiar? Giving in will delight your child but will cause both you and your child trouble in the long run. If you give in, your child will conclude that making demands is "good." Your preschooler is developing his moral compass based on the behaviors you permit, praise, and discuss in a positive way.

Artwork by Josh

Teach your rules

Since "good" and "bad" are absolute, you won't be surprised that your young child regards rules as absolute, too. That does not mean he likes them, just that they must be obeyed. Intentions and mitigating factors have no meaning.

SCENARIO

Recently potty-trained Matt was visiting his grandparents. They put on the sprinkler and told him to run through it.

"No!" He pulled back.

"It's fun," he was assured.

"No," he reiterated. "I can't get my underwear wet."

His bottoms were removed, and he ran through the water over and over, laughing joyously.

This is typical preschool thinking! If you are expected to keep your underwear dry, then they must always be kept dry. He could not consider either the overall condition of the underwear or how they became that way. A rule is a rule. Rather than try to explain to the child why the rule of keeping his pants dry does not apply in this situation, the adults wisely altered the situation so he would be happy running through the water.

As noted earlier, a belief that rules are absolute does not mean your preschooler will like your rules. Since no one likes to be told what to do (including you), you can expect your preschooler to scream in defiance and demand you change your rule, because unless you change it, it must be obeyed. But for your sanity, stand firm and teach your child responsible social behavior.

Your preschool-age child's belief that there is only one way of viewing things can be your ally. Enjoy your preschooler's view about rules, because all too soon your child will move to a higher level of thinking. Once he realizes that events and situations can be viewed more than one way, your rules will be scrutinized and criticized. If a friend's mother has a rule different from yours, your preschooler will argue the "rightness" of your rules, but as an elementary child, he will weigh the two rules and argue for the one that suits his interest.

The preschool child is learning to cooperate with peers and parents and is very interested in rules. You have been teaching your rules verbally and by correcting him when he does not obey. From these experiences your child has concluded that infractions of rules have consequences. Since your child does not factor in intent, if a sibling or peer breaks a rule, your child will feel the offender should be punished immediately—the harder the better. In this situation and other situations when the child's level of thinking will not enable him to comprehend an explanation based on a higher level of thinking, don't try to explain your decision. Just calmly restate your decision and acknowledge how your child feels about your decision. You don't have to get your child's approval. Calmly and pleasantly move on. Leave your explanation for when he has or is about to move to the next level of thinking. In just a few years, your child will understand intent and other components of more advanced thinking, and that is the time to teach them.

Ask your child to list your rules

If invited to do so, your preschool child will love to make a list of rules. They will be the ones you taught her, especially those that have gotten her into trouble. Later, as an elementary-age child, she will create original rules that fit her purposes, but as a preschooler, she will be listing the rules she knows. Thus, when you ask your three-year-old to "write" a list of rules, you are both reviewing your rules and enabling her to demonstrate that she has learned them. On the other hand, inviting your third grader to do the same may be counterproductive, as that will elicit some wild and self-serving rules that may require a firm parental response. Enjoy your preschooler's view on rules. Her views will change all too soon to suit you!

Preschool thinking can be the best ally you will ever have to instill your beliefs, goals, and rules. Since your child believes there is just one way of viewing things, he will accept your views. But once he reaches the next developmental stage, he will realize there are multiple ways of thinking about situations and will start questioning your rules and values. Expect to be challenged when he moves to the next level of thinking.

Walk through the Elementary School Years: Expanded Understanding

The exact age when your child moves into this more complex level of thinking will be determined by your child's internal timetable and, to some extent, her experiences. Celebrating her fifth or sixth birthday does not automatically change the way she thinks! Most elementary school tasks will require your child to engage in this more advanced thinking; therefore, if your child has not made this transition, she will benefit from starting elementary school a year later. Without this expanded way of thinking, your child will not understand many of the teacher's explanations. If your child is ready, or nearly ready, for this expanded thinking, start asking her questions that will encourage her to consider multiple points of views.

Love those knock-knock jokes

My favorite indicator that a child has moved from preschool thinking to a more expanded way of thinking is the appearance of jokes that have dual meanings. One such knock-knock joke goes as follows:

Knock knock.
Who's there?
Ada.
Ada who?
Ada burger for lunch.

Artwork by Rachel

The elementary-age child realizes that the sound "Ada" has dual meanings; it could be a name of a person and, when said quickly, sounds like "ate a." Since this ability to understand dual meanings is new to the child, she regards this type of joke as hilarious.

Another form of joke that often involves dual meanings is the classic question and answer. For example:

What do mosquitoes learn in art class?

They learn how to draw blood.

Our expanded thinker will laugh loudly and ask, "Get it? A mosquito draws blood to drink it, and the artist draws a picture of blood. Ha, ha! Get it? You can draw blood two ways. Ha, ha, ha!"

While you feel beat over the head, your elementary-age child thinks it is hilarious because, for the first time, he gets both meanings! Since this is a new skill, he feels a need to explain it to you just in case *you* don't get it. A preschool child would probably answer the previous joke with something like "paint," because the visual picture of a mosquito painting would be unexpected and thus funny. To the preschool child, an unusual visual experience is funny, because they judge things by how they look. Think about the illustrations you have seen in preschool workbooks and storybooks. An illustration aimed at preschool children—an elephant on skates or a child flying—creates visual images that contrast sharply with the real world, thus making them humorous.

On the other hand dual meaning jokes are humorous to your elementary-age child because, for the first time, he can consider two factors at the same thing. The next time you feel a moan coming on after hearing the thirteenth joke, give thanks that your elementary-age child has moved to this higher level of thinking. Take heart: once this skill is well-established, he will move on and will rarely tell these types of jokes. Humor is such a fun way to look at these two levels of thinking.

Expect expanded thinking

This new way of thinking enables your child to understand more concepts and events. Besides being able to consider multiple factors and views, your child sees and considers the change process (moving pennies or pouring water into a new glass). Your child can mentally manipulate objects and ideas. Your elementary school-age child is no longer confined by how things look at the moment. She can no longer be fooled into thinking she has as much milk in her skinny glass as her brothers have in their wide and tall glasses.

Remember the activity you did with your preschooler using pennies? She did not consider the change process. Now that your elementary child can consider the change process, she will understand the math teacher's explanation that the five chips used in addition remain five regardless of whether they are grouped in one pile or separated into piles of two and three or piles of one and four. The preschool child is capable of memorizing 2+3=5 but is unable to do the mental processing required to understanding that the total amount remains the same regardless of grouping. Initially your elementary-age child will learn by physically manipulating objects in math but will soon be able to mentally manipulate them.

Now that your elementary-age child is able to mentally see the change process, she will be able to tell you that the swing will return and will hit her if she runs in front of it. She won't always remember to use that thinking when she is engrossed in play and can, therefore, still run into the path of the swing, but she is now able to understand your explanation.

Your child can now consider multiple factors; therefore, he will be able to consider the opinions and intent of others. He will understand that some of his friends think differently than he does. He can consider multiple possible solutions and therefore do complex problem-solving tasks. Your parenting will change. You will discuss intent. You will involve your child more and more in the decisions related to the rules he must follow. A whole new world has opened up to you and your child.

Curtail tattling

Your elementary age believes that punishment must be administered quickly and harshly (to others, of course). Fairness becomes paramount at this age. Thus, if peers break a rule, it is only fair that they get in trouble. The adult must be told and must respond fairly by punishing the wrongdoers. Thus, tattling peaks at this age.

Of course, you want to know if one of your children is engaged in a dangerous activity. That is not tattling. Tattling is trying to raise the tattler's status by pointing out the misbehavior of another child. It is trying to be a co-parent and telling you what you should do. Tattling usually includes a demand to punish the other child. For example, if the tattler reported a sister was playing rather than doing homework, you could ask, "How is this helping your sister?" If the response is, "You told her to do her homework before she played," I would assure the tattler that *I* have a time when *I* will be checking on homework, and if it is not done, *I* will deal with it then. "This sounds like you are tattling so she will get in trouble. What could you do to help her? Ask her if she needs help."

Make it clear that your home is not only a "tattle-free home" but also a "help-others home." The goal of *reporting* is to *help* the other person. You will want your child to report actions that could result in harm to another person or to themselves. You will need to teach the distinction between tattling and helpful reporting.

During the elementary years, your child's behavior shifts from frequent tattling to peer cohesiveness, at which point a veil of secrecy prevails. You will not want your rejection of tattling to lead to the conclusion that sharing any information about a sibling or peer is inappropriate. As a preemptive strike against the peer secrecy of the late elementary age and adolescence, teach your early elementary-age child the difference between tattling and reporting information that will help someone. Discourage tattling, and praise reporting.

Prepare for an increase in peer influence

While your influence remains strong during the elementary school years, the influence of peers is becoming increasingly strong as well. Emerging peer loyalty contributes to an increased interest in team sports and other group activities. Behaviors or skills that contribute to the success of the team lead to popularity. Your child, at this age, will try to become a valued member of the team. This striving to belong gives the members of the group more power over your child than they had during the preschool years. Your child may give in to group pressure and engage in behaviors that you never expected. Your best defense is a good offense. Provide activities where he will succeed and develop a strong self-image. Help him cultivate friends whose behaviors and values are close to yours.

During the elementary school years, rule breaking, which is a refusal to be submissive to authority, can become a tool for getting peer recognition. Your child may conclude that the way to get the attention of his peers is to break the rules. Your cooperative, loving child may become defiant without apparent cause. At this point you can teach your child how your rules *help him* and keep him safe. He understands intent, use it to your advantage. What is the intent of the peer? What is your intent?

The importance of peers also gives rise to bullying. A child who bullies other children and forces submission often gains peer recognition. While bullies have been around for centuries, the impact of being bullied has recently come to light as investigations into school shootings often reveal that the shooter had been bullied most of his school life. Internet bullying is a new and dangerous problem.

The influence of peers will increase with each year from here on out. When you get to Path 9, play close attention to the section "Teach how to deal with others." Despite this increase in peer influence, you are still the most influential person in your child's life. Make the most of these years.

Path 5

Prevent Problems

There are things you can do to stop problems before they even start; i.e., be proactive. Initially it takes a great deal of energy and self-discipline, but in the long run, it makes parenting easier and more pleasurable. On this path you will learn that being predictable, being organized, having realistic expectations, and being a good communicator will reduce parenting problems. Granted, you can't totally eliminate problems, but you can diminish them.

Be Predictable

Be consistent

Consistency. The most important parenting skill is consistency. The second most important parenting skill is consistency. The third most important is—yes, you guessed it—consistency. Consistency is responding to your child's behavior with minimal variation. On Path 1 you listed your values and developed rules based on them. When your rules flowed from your values, your rules became consistent with each other. Now you need to be consistent in the way you respond to your child when she breaks those rules.

Inconsistency. The opposite of consistency—inconsistency—is allowing your child to engage in specific behaviors sometimes but not other times. Inconsistency can often occur when you permit a behavior not because of the needs of your child, but because your own:

- Preoccupation with your daily interests or events
- Lack of energy
- Present mood

Letting your child "get away" with misbehavior because you are on the phone, on the computer, or watching television will cause you problems later. Also, if you have "laid-back" days when you ignore his inappropriate behaviors and "crabby" days when nothing is permitted, you are being inconsistent.

SCENARIO

Sean: You don't have to finish that before we go outside.
Paige: Yes, I do.
Sean: What happens when you don't do what your parents tell you?
Paige: I have to do it.
Sean: But what if you don't?
Paige: You don't understand. I have to.
Sean: But what if you won't?
Paige: I told you, you don't understand. I have to.

In this scenario, both of the children were considering how their parents would respond to their refusal to obey. Both considered whether refusing was a reasonable choice. Since Paige's parents were consistent and since failure to comply brought not anger, but parental supervision that ensured compliance, she knew she had to complete the task before she would be permitted to play. Consistency requires you to put forth the energy necessary to ensure that your child follows your rules.

Consistency is important for three reasons. First, it promotes learning your rules. It provides all the conditions, discussed on Path 2, that make learning permanent. It provides feedback, which assures the behavior is practiced correctly, and repetition, which provides adequate time for the behavior to be learned.

Second, consistency allows your child to predict your response. If you have taught your rules and have been consistent in your follow-through, your child will be able to accurately predict your responses to specific behaviors, which will give him a better chance of keeping out of trouble. On the other hand, if he occasionally gets away with inappropriate behaviors, he will be less able to predict your response and more likely to get in trouble.

Third, consistency removes your child's need to determine what is permitted today. If "talking back" was ignored yesterday, your child will check to see if it is permitted today. You may have disliked tests when you were in school, but believe me, they were not nearly as distasteful as the continual testing your child will put you through if you are inconsistent!

I had the opportunity to observe the results of parental consistency when a family with three children under the age of five was visiting me. It was Christmas, and the tree lights were on. The two year old immediately went to the Christmas tree and touched an ornament. I asked the father if I should turn off the lights. In a calm voice, he told his son, "If you touch the ornaments, Mrs. B will have to turn off the lights." The two-year-old removed his hand and just stood there looking at the lights. There were no problems with the tree during the entire visit. If the father had used the common parent response of grabbing and scolding the child, I would have known the next few days would have been full of conflicts. But since the parenting was calm and consistent, the visit was delightful.

Being consistent initially requires extensive energy and follow-through, but in the long run it will make parenting easier and more enjoyable.

Be flexible

Flexibility. Consistency does not eliminate the need for you to be flexible. In fact, it mandates it! As stated previously, consistency is maintaining your life values. For example, you may value good health and regard adequate sleep as one way to support health. Since your three-year-old is going to need more sleep than your ten-year-old, they will have different bedtimes. Sleep needs require you to be flexible—i.e., have different bedtimes for the children in your family. While inconsistency is the failure to enforce a rule because doing so would be inconvenient for the parent, flexibility is adjusting the decision based on the needs of the child and to teach parental values. Being flexible is not the same as being inconsistent.

Rigidity. Consistency is not another term for rigidity. Rigidity is the opposite of flexibility. Rigidity is refusing to consider relevant information because you have already made up your mind. If you frequently enforce rules by saying, "Because I said so," you may be rigid. A rigid parent filters out relevant information about the situation or does not consider the child's level of development and personal characteristics. If new information or new insight would have led you to a different conclusion, you need to be flexible and change your decision to make it consistent with your values. Clearly explain the reason for the change and make it clear how the revised decision fits your expectations and is not letting the behavior slide. Being rigid is neither in your best interest as a parent nor in the best interest of your child. The parent who stubbornly sticks to a poor decision stifles good parent-child relationships and prevents the child from developing self-control. Rigidity is a major contributor to poor parenting.

Combine consistency and flexibility. When your child asks permission to do something or go someplace, avoid an immediate, knee-jerk *"no!"* Consider the situation. For example, if you have a rule requiring homework to be done before playing, and your child requests to delay homework until after supper, consider the child's past behavior. If the child is having trouble with that subject, you will probably tell her that she must do the homework before she plays. Period. End of discussion. If she has had a demanding day at school and you feel that she will be able to do her homework better if she takes a break, permit the delay and explain why. Or if she is doing well in school, you could say, "Yes, but I will use this to determine whether I can consider similar requests in the future." In this case, you are being flexible. You are adjusting your decision based on your goals of promoting both excellence in school and self-control. Your decisions should reflect both your parenting goals and the needs of your child.

Values. Consistency requires adherence to a basic underlying belief system and the rules you developed from it. Flexibility is making modifications for the benefit of the child and making your actions clearly reflect your beliefs, values, and standards. Both consistency and flexibility are essential elements of good parenting.

Be Organized

Organize your time

Organizing your time and your child's time is difficult. Don't fall into the trap of over-scheduling yourself or your child. A tired parent is not a happy parent. Don't stress your child with multiple activities. These days, it is not unusual for someone in the family to have a commitment every evening and for family meals to be "impossible." Are these activities really more important than having family time? Family life is, hopefully, lifelong. Don't shortchange it.

The way your family organizes its time, commitments, and living space gives your family its unique character. If you tested high in regularity in the earlier section where you reflected on your temperament, you have probably already developed family schedules and routines. Your home environment is probably already organized. If you tested low on regularity, you may have a flexible schedule and a casual physical environment. As you read about the impact of organization on your family life and your child, I hope you will find ways to adapt your present level of organization so it best serves each member of your family.

Establish a routine

A routine helps you deal with situations that trigger conflict, such as doing homework, completing a chore, or going to bed. A routine mentally prepares your child for the next activity and enables your child to be self-directed.

Like all approaches that reduce conflict in the end, this one, initially, requires a great deal of parental effort. From birth, your child has observed and participated in your family's routine. As soon as he is capable of cooperating with getting dressed and feeding himself, use parallel talking (words that describe what he is doing). This will teach the vocabulary he will need to understand your instructions. For example, you could say, "First we ate, and now we are going to brush our teeth." While observation is the initial and primary way your child will learn your routine, you will still need to frequently provide reminders. Since your child's ability will increase as he grows, teaching him your new expectations will be an ongoing task. If your child has learned your routine, these additional expectations will be easy to add.

A routine can tell your child what is coming next without your having to give a verbal reminder. The constant need for verbal reminders will probably irritate you and sound like nagging to your child. Also, the more you use verbal controls, the more opportunity there is for verbal combat. A routine enables your child to be self-directed and therefore reduces conflict.

Routines are especially valuable during times of transition; that is, when your child is going from one activity to another. Transition times, such as going from sleep to morning activities, going from home to school, and going from play to bed, can be difficult. Conflicts will be reduced if these times are handled the same way each day. First tell your child that the transition will occur in a five minutes. This will allow your child time to mentally adjust to the change.

For example, the following routine could be used to help your child adjust from sleep to morning activities:

1. Let the radio, set to automatically turn on at a specific time, be the signal to your child that he must get up in ten minutes.
2. A lamp on an automatic timer set for ten minutes later is the signal to put one's feet on the floor.
3. Walking to the bathroom may require your physical presence for some time.
4. The bathroom routine needs to be established. For the young child, put up a picture chart that shows the order in which she is to do each task. Take pictures of her and include her in selecting the pictures and telling you the order in which they go. This fun bonding activity not only teaches your expectations but also enables your child to be part of the planning process.
5. Have her get dressed in the clothes she laid out the night before. There is not enough time in the morning to decide what to wear (or to have a battle over it).
6. Next she comes to the kitchen for breakfast. Her backpack, packed the night before, is waiting for her by the door.

Your routine may be different from the one given here but, if getting ready for school or starting your day follows a consistent pattern, you will reduce morning conflicts.

A bedtime routine is vital for both adults and children. Both children and adults who have trouble sleeping are advised to go to bed and get up at regular times. While your child's bedtime routine may vary from the following one, adherence to a routine reduces bedtime conflicts. If, as a precaution against bedwetting or getting up during the night, you are cutting off liquids at a certain time, let your child know when that time has arrived and that this is her last chance to get a drink. A reminder of the upcoming bedtime helps your child mentally prepare herself. Do what works. Your bedtime routine could be as follows:

1. Start with a reminder that the bedtime routine begins when the present TV program is over or when the timer goes off in ten minutes.

2. Tell your child to select a book or books (not a game, which causes too much stimulation before bed). If your child uses finding a book as a way to delay going to bed, limit the time you will allow for this task by setting the timer for five to ten minutes.

3. Start the sequence for getting ready, such as washing the face, brushing teeth, and putting on pajamas.

4. Dim the lights. Tuck your child in bed and read one or more books.

5. Rub your child's back. Keep the lights dim and continue to play calming music or white noise after you leave the room.

If you consistently follow your routine, bedtime problems will gradually diminish.

Doing homework, another situation that often leads to conflict, will be less problematic if you have a set place and time for it. It can be right after school, right after a snack, or right after supper, but a time needs to be set. Otherwise your child is almost certain to say, "Not now!" when you mention homework. It also helps to have a specific time for your child to do chores. Don't nag about upcoming chores, but do remind your child that the chores must be done by a specific time. While verbal reminders often produce conflict, a chart that states the day and times for chores can reduce conflict.

If you and your child scored high on the temperament of regularity, establishing a routine will be easy for you. If your child scored low on regularity, this will be challenging. If you rated yourself low on regularity, creating this level of organization may be stressful, and you might want to make some modifications. As you parent, keep in mind the advantages of a routine, don't stress about it, and determine how it can be used to help your family.

Set the stage

Realtors tell potential home sellers to stage their homes so a potential buyer can envision herself living there. Likewise, you need to stage your home so your child can envision himself doing the activity permitted in each room in your home. The easiest nonverbal way to increase your child's independence or dependence, to encourage active or quiet play or to calm or stimulate him is to organize a room or a space in a way that encourages the behavior you want.

You can increase your child's independence by buying shoes and clothing that are easy to put on and take off, and by provide hooks or rods at your child's level for hanging his clothing. If your child can reach his own clothes and put them on without your help, he most likely will. Store plastic drinking glasses and plates in a lower drawer or shelf in the kitchen so your child can get a drink and snack. Also provide stools, if needed, to enable your child to reach the sink. If he can reach his own drinking glass and get water from the refrigerator door or sink, he most likely will. After all, children like to feel grown-up. If everything is beyond his reach and he needs your help to hang up his coat or to get a drink, you are encouraging dependence. How you organize your home will promote either independence or dependence.

Set the stage for both active and quiet play. Your child needs places, both inside and outside, where he can be active and can use up that energy without getting in trouble for it. Inside, you could provide your preschooler with blocks, imaginative dress-up clothes, and cars. Your older child could have chin-up bars as well as technology-based games and television games that require him to get up and move. Everyone in the family could make good use of mats and low balance beams. Outside, your child needs a place to ride trikes or bikes, play ball, and engage in running games and sports. You may need to schedule a time to take him to a park where he can do these things. Providing a place to be active makes it easier to be quiet at other times and in other places.

Your child also needs a place, inside and outside, to be quiet. Puzzles and art materials are great for all ages. Select an easy-to-clean supervised location for the art activities. All ages need an inviting place to read, such as pillows close to a bookcase or a large basket filled with books.

Your child needs stimulation, but not so much that he is bouncing off the walls. How much stimulation (and how much calming) your child needs depends greatly on his temperament. Your choice of colors, pictures, and toys can stimulate or calm your child. Your highly active child will need an area free from bright colors and interesting toys when doing homework. His bedroom needs to be free of stimulating toys and sounds. Your quiet child, on the other hand, will need bright colors and toys that will stimulate interaction.

If there is no designated place for a toy, it will find its way to the middle of the room. Organize the play area and have a place to store everything. Rotating books and toys can improve order by reducing the number of items out at a given time. If your child does not play with the returned item, it is probably time to store it for your next child or give it away.

As your child matures, his interests and needs change. Removing the outgrown toys will be less upsetting if your child is included in making the decision. Your child could create room for upcoming birthday or Christmas presents by selecting toys to donate to a toy drive or to sell when you have a yard sale.

A feeling of ownership will increase your child's willingness to help keep the area organized. His area may be a room or a space identified by a small throw rug. Regardless of the size of the space, include your child in the decision-making. Selecting his rug or bedspread increases the feeling of ownership.

You are the set director. Organize your home in a way that clearly tells your child what can be done and where it can be done.

Prepare for changes

There will be changes in your life that will require you to make extensive changes. One of those is the arrival of a new family member, often a new baby.

Reorganize before the baby arrives. Try to make the changes that will most affect your older child before the baby arrives. For example, if sleeping arrangements need to be changed to accommodate your new baby, make these changes a month or more beforehand so that your older child will not blame the baby for them.

Help your older children develop realistic expectations. Before your baby arrives, reduce the probability of jealousy by helping your older child develop realistic expectations. If your older child expects the baby to be a playmate or does not realize the baby will require a great deal of your time, the reality of having a baby in the home can devastate him.

Plan to give extra attention to the older child. The birth of another child creates new challenges. The needs and interests of the older sibling(s) haven't changed, so try and keep their lives as normal as possible. Express your love for them and give them a lot of attention. If an older sibling is a toddler or preschooler, suggest that family members who are bringing a baby gift also bring a small gift for the older child.

Plan how your older child, depending on her developmental level, can help with the baby. A young sibling can fetch the needed diaper. Sitting on your lap or next to you, your older child may be able to hold the baby. You can find ways to let your child assist in feeding, bathing, or entertaining your baby. Let the older child share a book with the baby.

If she can read, encourage her to read to the baby. A sibling too young to hold the infant can be given a baby doll to feed and bathe when Mom feeds and bathes the baby. Be creative in incorporating your older child into the care of the baby.

Plan activities that you can do with both the baby and the older child. For instance, you can include both of them when you read a book, take a walk, sing, or play with toys. Positive shared experiences will help your children develop positive feelings toward each other.

Regression, which is common and a plea for attention, is a reversal to an earlier stage of development. For example, your child may stop using the potty and require diapering even though he has been potty-trained for several months. He may restart thumb-sucking. Provide attention for his age-appropriate behavior and take care of his regressed behaviors in a matter-of-fact manner. Remember, your older child needs one-on-one time with you. The following scenario is an example of a plea for attention and a fleeting consideration to regress.

SCENARIO

Each time Mom started to feed the baby, Shawn, who had recently been potty-trained, requested to be taken to the potty.

Mom took Shawn to the potty just before the next feeding. Within minutes she heard Shawn call out, "Potty, potty" as he jumped up and down and grabbed himself. Holding the baby in one arm, she helped Shawn with this newly acquired skill of using the potty.

Before the next feeding, Mom took Shawn to the potty and told him to go now, as she was not going to take him while feeding the baby. As soon as the feeding began, Shawn called out, "Potty, potty" as he jumped up and down and grabbed himself.

> "Later. Now you can sit next to me." Mom continued to feed the baby. Shawn stood there, looking up at Mom as he calmly urinated on the floor. Mom ignored him.
>
> Before the next feeding, Mom took Shawn to the potty and told him to go now, as she was not going to take him until she was through feeding the baby. As soon as the feeding began, Shawn called out, "Potty, potty" as he jumped up and down and grabbed himself.
>
> "Later. Now you sit next to me." Mom continued to feed the baby, and Shawn crawled up next to her. She kissed him on the forehead.

When the baby arrived, Shawn, like many children, used a behavior that worked when he was younger; i.e., he temporarily regressed. The manipulative behavior stopped as soon as Shawn discovered it did not work. No attention was given when he urinated on the floor, because even a scolding would be attention, and attention was what he wanted (see Path 8, "Ignore attention-getting behaviors"). Attention was given when he exhibited the positive behavior of sitting next to Mom and the baby. Had the behavior worked, he would have continued to use infantile behavior, which would have been true regression. Since it didn't work, he regressed only briefly. How long your older child's regression will last is determined by how persistent he is in general and how you respond to his regression. Don't let it work; give him attention when he exhibits age-appropriate behavior. A behavior that doesn't work will stop.

Sibling rivalry can escalate to sibling abuse or sibling bullying. To prevent this, clearly state the behavior you expect. Don't ignore verbal or physical attacks. Promote positive sibling relationships by spending individual time with each of your children.

Be Realistic

Expect your child to do what he or she can do, no more and no less

Unrealistically high expectations will cause discipline problems and will cause your child to stop trying. On the other hand, if you don't have any expectations, your child will not be motivated to try.

When your expectations are developmentally appropriate, your child will be able to meet them, and that will increase his self-confidence. As your child matures and his thinking, social, communication, and motor skills increase, so should your expectations. For example, an infant's hunger cry should be met with milk, but the toddler's cry and pointing for milk should not. Rather, the child should be required to use a pleasant voice and sounds or words he can make, whether it is only "mmm" for milk or "ding" for drink. On the other hand, the toddler shouldn't be expected to sit as long at the dinner table as a four-year-old. Your elementary-age child can be required to load the dishwasher. Having achievable expectations teaches your child to set and reach achievable goals.

If you expect your child to do something before he is developmentally ready, you are in for a lot of conflict and frustration. When your child can't meet your expectations, you are setting him up for failure. In that case, he will either become confrontational or give up and become an underachiever.

Likewise, parents who have low expectations raise low achievers. Parents whose expectations are based on their careful observations and accurate assessment of their child's ability have high-achieving and motivated children. Ask yourself: am I expecting too much for his age, or am I letting him get by with immature behavior?

When your family is made up of children of different ages, your expectations will have to be different for each child. Age-appropriate expectations are guaranteed to bring forth complaints of "Unfair!" from siblings. (Review the section on flexibility.) Having the same expectations for all ages is what is unfair (review the section on rigidity). Point out the "advantages" and "disadvantages" of each age. Explain, but don't get drawn into an argument. When my son asked me, "Why do I have to do that?," I told him, "Because it needs to be done, and you are capable of doing it."

For your child's sake, expect your child to do what he can do—no more and no less.

Your child deserves to be liked

No one likes being around a loud, demanding child or a clinging, whining child—not even the parent! As the parent, you may love your difficult child but not really like her. Your child deserves not only to be loved but also to be liked! You may feel that by not correcting your child, you are showing love. However, you will end up unhappy, and the unhappiest person will be your child.

No child should be put in the position of feeling disliked simply because the parent hasn't put forth the effort to teach her socially acceptable behavior. Don't let the child, or those around you, convince you that just letting your child do her own thing is an act of love. It is not. Love requires you to teach your child appropriate behavior. On Path 1, when I gave a warning to the laid-back parent, I told you about a parent who let her children walk all over her. I'm sure you also know parents like that and have observed that it is the child who suffers. Love is spending the energy and time necessary to teach appropriate behavior. It is hard work, but no one likes an out-of-control child, and your child deserves to be liked.

Mirror, mirror on the wall

Tell me about yourself. Who are you? What kind of person are you? How did you develop that self-image? My self-image of being friendly grew from what other people said to me and how they treated me. Other people are mirrors that influence your—and your child's—self-image.

SCENARIO

A kindergartner and his second-grade brother scurried down the street after getting off the school bus. Their mother stood on the porch, and, as the children started to cross their yard, she called, "Come here! Let me see if you are as cute as you were when you left for school this morning." She smiled at the second-grader as she cupped his face in her hands.

"Yes, you are just as cute as you were this morning."

She stood quietly waiting for the younger child, who was playing as he took the last steps home. He came up to her, and she cupped his face in her hands and said, "Yes, you are just as cute as you were this morning."

I happened to be outside when those neighbor children arrived home from school. The message "You are important to me" was very powerful. What a great mirror the mother was. What a great way to build a positive self-image. No wonder those children are so likeable.

Like the mother in the scenario, you are your child's most important mirror. You tell her who she is with your words and actions. How do you describe your child to others? I am amazed when I observe a parent or a teacher talk about a child—with the child standing nearby—as though she were not there or could not hear. Your child certainly hears what is said about her and incorporates that into her self-image. If you describe your child as loud and boisterous, your child will live up to your expectations and be loud and boisterous. If you describe her as loving and cooperative, your child will incorporate that into her self-image and will be loving and cooperative.

Not every mirror is reliable. Just as some mirrors have imperfections that distort a person's image, the feedback your child receives from others can be distorted. Teach your child that not everything people say about her is an accurate reflection of who she is. Bullies are the worst distorters of a person's self-worth, so don't let your child get her self-image from the bully's belittling (see Path 10, "Rebuff that bully"). Tell your child that the bully is distorting her reflections because he wants her to feel insignificant so she will be afraid of him. Like the big bad wolf in the fairy tale, he distorts (lies) as a way of controlling and scaring others. Use only reliable mirrors!

Be a Good Communicator

Listen up before you speak up

Good communication involves both active listening and controlled response. If you and your child develop good communication skills, you will reduce your child's conflicts with you, his siblings, and his friends.

Active listening

Active listening promotes language development by encouraging your child to talk. It requires you to demonstrate, through words and body language, that you have heard what he is saying, care about what he says, and respect how he feels about it. Active listening requires you to do the following:

- Listen carefully so you can detect your child's feelings.
- Reflect those feelings back to your child using carefully chosen words.

- Rephrase, but don't parrot, what your child has said.
- Ask nonjudgmental questions that will encourage your child to continue the discussion.
- Use positive nonverbal communication, such as smiling, when talking to your child.
- Get down to your child's eye level; that is, sit on the floor or a chair.
- Maintain eye contact throughout the discussion.
- Reflect empathy with your facial expressions.
- Stop what you are doing and sit quietly as you listen to your child.
- Lean slightly toward your child.

Active listening can keep your child talking, help you learn what is going on in your child's life, and let your child know you care about him. Productive reflecting on a situation that is loaded with emotions takes time, so be patient and give your child time to process both the experience and your reflection of it. If he already has the skills he needs to resolve the problem, then active listening may help him realize that he can resolve this problem on his own. On the other hand, if he is telling you about a problem that requires advice or a complex solution, you will find that the techniques discussed on Path 9 ("Teach how to deal with others") are more appropriate.

Avoid nonverbal expressions of disapproval, such as frowning, shaking your head, crossing your arms, and turning your head away from your child. Nothing communicates disinterest more than continuing with your task as your child talks to you. Good communication takes time, but it is essential for building a positive relationship with your child.

Make your home a "words-only" home

How does your child let you know what she wants? Crying? Whining? Hitting? I am sure you find those approaches irritating! You will want to replace those irritating behaviors with words.

If you ignore requests made in an inappropriate manner, those approaches will cease. You need to require age-appropriate words and voice tones. For example, tell your child that your home is a words-only home and that only requests made in a pleasing voice will be *considered.* Inform your child that crying and whining requests cannot be *considered.* Tell her, "Next time, ask in a pleasant voice."

If your child immediately makes the same request using a pleasant voice, tell her that the previous behavior eliminates all possibility of this request being *considered* at this time. Inform your child that if she had used a pleasant voice initially, you would have *considered* the request. Tell your child to use a pleasant voice next time. End of discussion. Do not get pulled into a confrontation.

Why not consider the request as soon as your child stops crying or his tone of voice changes? Simple. There is a psychological principle called "chaining." When you let a behavior work (reinforce a specific behavior), your child concludes that everything he did leading up to your agreement contributed to his final success. You would be teaching that first you whine or cry to soften up your parent; *then* you ask. You want the *first* request to be in a pleasant voice, right?

If your child returns twenty or thirty minutes later and uses a pleasing voice, consider the request. First, compliment her on remembering that your home is a words-only home. Hopefully, the request is one you can grant. If not, tell your child you are proud of the way she asked and explain the reason for the refusal. Your smile and your approval are the best reward possible for your child. Learning to ask for things in an appropriate way teaches your child that words, used appropriately, are useful.

Teach words to reduce conflict

Social interactions bring both fun and conflict. Since conflict will occur, teach your child to use words to express himself. You taught your child that words are useful by giving him water only when he said "wa-wa" or "dink." Now teach him that words are useful when interacting with friends. When your preschool child is dealing with people closer to his size, he will be tempted to shove, hit, or bite to get his way. If it works, he will continue. If your child hits his friend or grabs his toy, tell your child, "Use your words. Ask him to give you the truck when he is through." He will tell you that he wants it *now*. Say, "Now you can play with a ball or your blocks. Later you can play with the truck." You may need to play with the other toy to entice your child to try it. You will need to calmly and persistently instruct your child to ask for toys rather than just grabbing them. Teaching your child to use words to resolve conflicts is much harder than teaching him to say "wa-wa" when he wants a drink. It requires more time, a great deal of wisdom, and plenty of patience, but it is worth it.

If your child bites, do not bite him back nor tell other children to bite back. This only models biting as a way of expressing disapproval. You want to replace this inappropriate way of communicating with a socially acceptable expression, namely, appropriate words. That will happen only if you teach your child the words you want him to use. If another child takes your child's toy and your child responds by biting, tell your child to say, "I don't like that. I want my toy back." You will have to guide both children through the conflict so they understand that force is not an acceptable way to solve a dispute. Learning to use words decreases your child's need to communicate by crying, hitting, biting, and grabbing.

Emotions denied are intensified

Have you ever been unable to find just the right words to express your feelings? Probably. It's easier to attach words to what you see than to how you feel. Yet nothing increases physical conflict more than a person's inability to use words to accurately express feelings. If left unexpressed or expressed in a verbally confrontational way, emotions will intensify. Teach her how to express her emotions.

You teach words used to express feelings in the same way that you teach other words. On Path 4 you learned that language skills develop easily when you provide language activities at the developmentally appropriate level. Now you can apply those same principles to the teaching of words that express feelings.

Just as you teach the word "ball" by saying "ball" as he is playing with one (that is, you do parallel talking), you teach words that express emotions by using that word when he exhibits that emotion. When he screams, say, "Mad. Brandon mad." When your older child is having an emotional meltdown, you can model an appropriate statement he can use in lieu of that behavior.

Early utterances are one-word sentences followed by two-word sentences, and finally complex sentences and expanded statements. Likewise, you will teach words that convey emotions in a planned way. Start with a single word. When your child is using two-word sentences, you will use two-word sentences to describe his feelings. Continue to expand the length of your examples to meet the needs of your elementary-age child. Each time your child confronts you, the words you use and your reactions to him model how to respond when he is provoked.

If your child is told that it is bad to be angry or sad, she will just suppress those feelings, and when they are expressed at a later time, they will be stronger than they were originally. On the other hand, if you teach your child the words for her emotions, she will learn to use words to express her feelings, and she won't resort to an emotional meltdown in order to communicate how she feels. Emotions denied are intensified.

Path 6

Provide Powerful, Positive Parenting

Rule Out Problems

Mind reading not required

Your child is not a mind reader. Neither is he born knowing how to become a cooperative member of your household—or any other household for that matter! Reasonable rules will help your child learn your expectations.

1. Determine what rules you want for your home.
2. Make simple rules that your child can understand.
3. Teach your rules to your child.

Determine rules. Your rules need to be based on the values you wrote down as you went down Path 1. They need to be appropriate for your child's level of development and temperament as well as appropriate for your family's lifestyle. If one of your values (life guides) is to respect the environment, you need to determine how you will maintain your home environment. Based on that value, you may develop a rule: "You may play with your toys in the family room." Where your child can play with his toys is your decision, but the child has a right to know where he can play and not get in trouble for having toys at that location.

Understandable rules. Your rules need to be few, generalizable across situations, and understandable. The fewer rules you have, the easier it will be for your child to remember them, and keeping rules general allows you to get by with fewer rules. Look over the rules you wrote down. If you have created a long list of dos and don'ts, group similar ones together. For example, putting toys away, putting clothes into the clothes hamper, and loading or unloading the dishwasher could all be based on the value of respecting the environment and the rule of putting everything where it belongs. Since you are teaching him to apply your rules to various situations, he will be able to apply them to situations he encounters when you are not around.

Teach rules. You need to systematically teach your rules. Earlier I explained that repetition spread over time makes learning permanent. After your initial teaching of the rules, you will repeat them often and over time as you correct your child's behavior. I also explained earlier that consistency improves learning, because it enables you to teach and reteach your expectations. Your child will not learn your rules after being told a single time. If rules change frequently your child will never learn them. Teaching your rules can be exasperating! However, you will be less frustrated with your constant need to restate them if you view each inappropriate behavior as another opportunity to teach your expectations. Praise your child when she follows the rules. Your child has a right to know your family rules and how to apply them so she can live calmly and securely in her home.

Artwork by Rachel

State expectations clearly and in positive terms

Do you know a hard-to-please person? You do one thing and they criticize it. You try something else, only to be criticized again. You probably concluded that they couldn't be pleased. Why bother trying? It is quite possible that they were not specific enough because they really didn't know what would please them. You must decide what behaviors will please you, and then tell your child what those behaviors are. Once you've stated what you expect, you are committed to accepting that behavior. *Be specific.*

SCENARIO

Mom, Dad, and Ryan were waiting to cross the street. Mom reached out to take Ryan's hand. He twisted and pulled away. She leaned over to grab him, and he scooted to the opposite side of the walk. Again she tried to grab him, but he eluded her.

Mom said, "You must take someone's hand. I don't care whose, but you must hold someone's hand as we cross the street."

Ryan held up his left hand, pointer finger fully extended. He grabbed his own finger with his right hand. He extended both arms and held them at eye level so everyone could clearly see he had taken "someone's" hand—his own.

Obviously, the mother in the previous scenario did not mean anyone's hand: she meant any adult's hand. Unless your instructions are extremely clear, your child will interpret them in a way that allows him to continue doing just what he wants to do. She needed to clearly restate her expectation. She could have said, "You must take either my hand or your dad's hand." Make your instructions clear and specific.

Telling your child the behavior you want is extremely effective. If you are like most parents, you have little experience observing or using this technique. The next time you start to tell your child, "Don't do that," stop yourself and tell her what you want her to do (e.g., "use a pleasant voice when you talk to your brother"). Rather than scold your child (e.g., "stop tracking in mud"), tell her what you want ("take your shoes off before you come in and put them on that throw rug"). Nothing makes life run more smoothly than deciding what behaviors you want and telling your child, in positive terms, what you want her to do.

Increase expectations gradually

Start teaching your expectations when your child is a toddler. As your child grows, gradually increase your expectations and decrease your reminders. For example, when teaching him to pick up his belongings, start when he is a toddler by handing him one toy and telling him where it should go. Once this is easy, give him two toys and tell him where each should go. As he grows, increase the number of instructions he needs to remember from one to two and then two to three. You could say, "Put your dirty clothes in the clothes hamper, your shoes along the closet wall, and stand up all the books on the shelves." As his understanding develops, tell him to clean up his room and then let him do it on his own. If you start your expectations when he is a toddler and gradually increase them as he goes through elementary school, you will eventually be able to have a standing rule that his room must be cleaned by noon on Saturday, or there will be a consequence such as no phone or no technological "toys" for the remainder of the day. No reminder. With age-appropriate expectations, age-appropriate support, consistency, and practice, your child can be taught to be a cooperative member of your household.

Look! I did it!

If you are like me, you need to keep a chart or a calendar where you write down your responsibilities for the week. My chart is my lifeline. Your child will also benefit from having a weekly or monthly chart. For your older children, your expectations can be in writing, but, as described earlier, your child who cannot read will need a picture chart.

Provide stickers your child can put on her weekly chart or calendar each time she completes a task. Encourage your child to use the stickers on her own, but provide help if needed. The more she does on her own, the more successful she will feel. Nothing beats the feeling of success.

You can make charting easy by putting it on the computer. There are many options, such as a calendar that comes with your computer or phone, or you can make a template to use repeatedly. This eliminates the need to retype the tasks that remain the same week after week. You can post each child's chart in her room and also make one for the entire family with each person's responsibilities and activities printed in a different color. For example, everything Robert has to do could be printed in blue. When he sees "feed the dog" in blue in the 7:00 a.m. slot, he is reminded that he must feed the dog before he goes to school. Put the days of the week across the top and time slots, by hours, down the side. This global picture of your family's week will also be very helpful to you or any helper, such as a grandparent or babysitter. The chart serves as a visual reminder of the complexities of organizing your entire family.

Charting serves as an effective, parent-free reminder. Initially, it requires adult supervision, but the goal is to have your child complete the tasks on her own. When initially teaching your child how to use the chart, you may need to give or withhold rewards. You might give a specified amount of money for a given task, or you could do the opposite and deduct money from the allowance if the chores listed on the chart are not done. For example, if your child has not unloaded the dishwasher by noon, she will lose one dollar of her allowance. If it is not unloaded by 1:00 p.m., she will lose another dollar. If losing allowance money is not effective with your child, select a consequence that matters to her, like no dessert after supper or the loss of phone, computer, or television privileges. Carefully select rewards and consequences based on your child's interests. Don't nag. Don't yell. The fewer words exchanged, the more effective this method will be. Consequences for noncompliance should be automatic and must result in losing something the child *wants*. When your child uses the chart without being reminded, compliment her on her dependability.

Charting can be a good parenting technique for all parents, but it is especially useful for the following types of parents:

- Parents who have a complex schedule;
- Parents who dislike verbal confrontations and, therefore, ignore behavior rather than confront it (charting reduces verbal interaction);
- Parents who get angry easily and, therefore, are easily pulled into a verbal argument;
- Parents who rank themselves either very high or very low on the temperament of regularity (see Path 3, "Discover your child's temperament").

Your family's chart will be different from your neighbors'. It will include responsibilities suited for the age of your child and the needs of your family.

Remember the "wet paint" principle

When you see a sign that reads "Wet Paint," are you tempted to touch it to see if the paint is still wet? The sign plants an idea. When you tell a child not to engage in a specific behavior, like touching items in the store, you are calling attention to that behavior and increasing the likelihood that he will do it. Tell your child what behavior you want, such as "Put your hands in your pocket and look with your eyes."

SCENARIO

Sean had used clay to make a present for each person in the family. When finished, he put the presents under a large bowl. On top of the bowl, he put a sign that said, "Stay out. Do not look."

A short time later, his sister walked by, looked at the sign, and lifted the bowl.

"Stop! Didn't you see the sign?" Sean called out.

With a grin, his sister replied, "Yeah. That's why I decided to look!"

Lifting the bowl and looking under it is so typical of human behavior. The "don't look" sign spurred the sister's curiosity. I remember watching a demonstrated lesson on creative movement where the teacher said, "Now remember, don't hit your neighbor." The little boy sitting in front of me reached over and lightly punched his neighbor. An idea had been planted.

The goal is to call attention to the behavior you want. "I liked the way you put your plate in the sink" is a clue to the siblings to do likewise. "Your beautiful smile tells me that you are doing a good job brushing your teeth" will encourage him to continue brushing his teeth and will encourage siblings to also brush more regularly. Likewise, saying, "OK, you two. Stop shoving" says to the other children, "Look at the two shoving each other." The observer may think that the jostling looks like fun and decides to do it now or later. Instead, tell the boys what you want them to do, such as "Use this ball for a game of catch."

The "wet paint principle" says that the behavior we call attention to will probably be tried. Since your child will do the behaviors you call attention to, make this principle work for you: call attention to the behaviors you want.

Anticipate and Act

Prepare for the brewing storm

If a storm is brewing, do preventive planning. Keep it from becoming full-blown. Some situations, like long car trips and shopping, frequently trigger conflict between children. If your child is highly active and easily excitable, playtime may frequently end in disaster. As you observe your child, you will discover what triggers conflicts with you or with his peers. Take preventive action before the conflict flares.

If car trips inevitably lead to backseat fighting, plan some interventions before you go. Plan word games, take hand-held computer games or a small television. Take a camping potty or a container with a tight lid to use as an emergency potty. You know which of your kids are most likely to pick on each other, so separate them. Think ahead.

Going to the grocery store can be a disaster. Before you go, decide if your child can walk by your side or must sit in the cart. Announce your decision ahead of time. Your decision could be, "You may walk by me if you hold onto the cart, but you will have to sit in the cart if you wander off." Once you make your decision, stick to it. Have your child help you make your grocery list. Your young child can cut out pictures of the food items you plan to purchase and paste them on a piece of paper. Older children can write all or part of the list for you. Consider dividing the list and giving part of the list to your child. The person with that listed item will get to put it into your grocery cart, or even his cart if the store provides child-size carts. You may decide to allow your child to select one item. If so, inform your child before you go of the parameters of his choice. You could leave the choice open-ended or select the type of food, like one fruit. When your child says, "Can I buy this?," ask, "Is this the one thing you want to buy, or do you want to look some more? We can come back to this aisle if this is the one thing you want." This will keep your child actively thinking as well as teach him that choices must be made, because you cannot buy everything he wants.

Your impending storm may be caused by your child's temperament. If your child is impulsive and has control issues, you will need to increase her self-control by carefully planning brief experiences where she can work on self-control. If playtime with peers often results in conflict, don't avoid playtimes, but do make them short, provide cool-down times, and set simple rules as described in the next section, "Know how to stop before you start."

If there is a storm brewing at your home, think of ways to reduce it before it becomes full-blown.

Know how to stop before you start

Laughing and playing with your child is one of the joys of parenting, but playtime can become a disaster if you are ready to stop before your child is.

SCENARIO

Mommy and four-year-old Bobby were laughing, running, and playing with a soccer ball. They threw it and kicked it. For fifteen minutes the air was full of laughter. A smiling mother announced, "I'm tired. Enough playtime."

"*No*! I want to play some more." Bobby pushes Mommy.

"Be careful," she scolded gently. "I'm too tired to play."

Bobby continued to run around and kick the ball. He jumped on Mommy's back. "Bobby, don't be so rough," Mommy instructed. The game had become too physical. Bobby was laughing, running, and having a great time.

"Time to stop," Mom announced again. "Stop! Stop it!"

Bobby ran around in circles and called out, "Let's play! Let's play. Catch it, Mommy" The ball hit Mom in the face. Mom grabbed Bobby and screamed, "Go to your room!" Bobby started crying, and Mommy went to put an icepack on her swollen cheek.

I am sure that you, too, have wondered how a game with your child or a group of children that started out so great could end so poorly. Maybe, like this mother, you just need to teach how to stop an activity before you start it. If you know that an activity is going to stimulate and excite your child, you need to set boundaries, decide how you will stop the activity, and teach your stop signals.

All professional games have rules and signals that the officials—umpires, referees—use to control the game. You need them, too. As the parent, you may be both the game official and a player. No professional football, basketball, or baseball game simply goes on until the players decide they want to stop! These games have time limits. You may determine ahead of time how long your game will last or what behaviors will result in stopping the game. Remember, you are going to get tired before your child. Try a shorter time initially until you learn more about your level of endurance and your child's response to the calls of the official (that's you). You can always play a second game or make future ones longer. It is wise to stop while play is going smoothly. A well-officiated game with clear boundaries will end well.

You need signals to control the game and stop it. Don't plan to control the game by yelling, as that just increases the noise and encourages the children to yell louder. If you and your child have a favorite sport, use the signals of that sport. Your child already knows them and understands how they keep the game going smoothly. You can also use a signal such as "freeze." For example, if you plan to use "freeze" to stop the activity, start by practicing freezing. Tell the children you are going to show the freeze signal and that you will look for people who freeze quickly. Name *everyone* who freezes. If you only recognize the first person, you are teaching the group that unless you freeze first, there is no need to freeze. Initially stop after a short—very short—time of play. Do a deep breathing activity or sing a song to calm the child or children. Once they are calm, let play resume.

Whether you are engaged in active play with just your child or you are supervising a group of your children's friends, you need to set the time limit for the activity and establish the control signals before the interactions begin. It is important to teach how to stop before you start!

Provide time for just the two of you

What your child wants more than any toy or any snack is time with you. Nothing is more flattering to a child (or an adult) than learning someone finds us so desirable that he or she wants to spend time with us.

You may be wishing for more time *with* or more time *away* from your child. If your child clings and demands your attention, you may feel you need less time together. However, your child's behavior is a plea for your undivided attention. Ten minutes of one-on-one time with you may reduce the clinging behavior that drains you physically and emotionally.

If you work outside the home, before you rush in to pick up your child at the day care or after-school care center, take time to sit in the car and listen to a couple of songs on the radio. Practice a deep breathing routine. I can hear you laugh at that suggestion. I know you don't have time, but I am telling you, it will save time—the time you spend to recoup will be time you don't have to spend in conflict with your child. When you go in, get down to your child's eye level and look at her papers with her. If you are picking up more than one child, take time in each room to let that child tell you about her work. Move slowly and calmly. On the way home, use the time in the car to focus on your child and her interests. This thirty-minute slowdown will save you time in the long run and reduce conflicts. When you get home, include the child in getting the meal ready. Let her get the plates and silverware out of the dishwasher and put them on the table.

Schedule time with your child when she won't have to compete for your attention. If you read a story and give a backrub to each of your children at bedtime, going to sleep will be more palatable for them and will give you one-on-one time with each of them. Your child loves you and wants time with you.

Watch for contagious behaviors

Colds and measles are not the only things that are contagious—so are behaviors. Your child will "catch" your behaviors and the behaviors of others in his environment. Watch your child interact with peers. Do you hear phrases you frequently use? Do you see your behaviors or the behaviors of other family members? Probably so. These reenactments of us can trigger an awareness of behaviors we need to change. You may be tempted to tell your child, "Do what I say, not what I do." You were probably told that. Did it work? Probably not. Your child will do what you *do*.

The most effective way to teach your values is to reflect them in the way you live your life. You do not need to set aside a special time to teach concern for others. As you show concern for your family and community, you are teaching your values. Live your values. If you do, you can rest assured that they are reflected in your actions and that your values will be caught.

Respond Appropriately to Appropriate Behaviors

Decide which behaviors you want to work

One thing is certain: your child is not dumb! She quickly discovers what works with you and what doesn't.

SCENARIO

Marsha told her friend, "I will need to get my dad's permission to go with you. Don't worry when he says 'no.' He always does, but in the end, I'll get to go."

As expected, he said "no," and after hearing repeated utterances of "*Pleeeease,*" he sent Marsha to her mom. This, as predicted, was brief. She was sent back to her dad. She informed him that her mom said it was up to him. The pleading restarted, and, looking disgusted and exhausted, he said, "Okay, okay!"

"See," said Marsha. "I knew I'd be able to go if I just kept at it. Pleading always works."

I doubt that her parents enjoyed this interaction, but it worked, so it continued. Children are smart and quickly learn what works. As you were growing up, what worked in your home? Who was the easy touch? Who was the decider? How did you use this knowledge?

Take a look at your interactions with your child. What is the decision-making process? Are the behaviors that work with you ones that will also work with a teacher or a boss? If not, revise how you want your child to approach you. Explain what will work with you. Children do what works. If you don't like what your child is doing, then stop letting it work!

"Catch" your child being good

Don't miss the good things your child does! We tend to see only what we look for. If you look for your child's misbehavior so you can punish it, you will see it. If you look for your child's good behavior so you can praise it, you will see it.

Some children are innately more resistant to following direction and may be labeled willful or difficult. Even those children have brief moments of being delightful! Lay in wait and catch him in that rare cooperative (or more cooperative) moment. Don't let it slip by unnoticed. Let your child bask in a moment of total acceptance as the two of you enjoy the moment laughing together. When you have "caught" your child being good, please don't ask the child, "Why can't you be like this more often?" That will reinforce your child's self-image of being a troublemaker.

Looking for the child's good behavior is *not* the same as refusing to see nonadaptive or inappropriate behaviors. I have already discussed the inappropriateness of allowing antisocial behaviors to go unchecked and reminded you that every child deserves to be liked. Do catch your child being good. That will promote the self-image of "I am a good child" and increase socially responsible behaviors. Praise can be powerful.

Aundrea's Book
Kindergarten

Artwork by Aundrea

Make your praise powerful

A trainer of support dogs told her television interviewer that over the years trainers had learned that using only praise enables the dogs to learn quickly and produces a dependable dog. They had, therefore, stopped using any form of punishment. They also found that praise produced more reliable behavior than treats. Praise produces results in people, too.

Punishment identifies what you do not want. Praise identifies what you *do* want. Praise is most powerful when it is perceived as genuine, specifies why the behavior is praiseworthy, and is used frequently but not continually. Praise followed by a qualifier is not praise. "You did a good job, but…" is criticism. Preceding a critical evaluation with praise does not soften the criticism; it just reduces the power of future praise from that person. Your child will just wait for the "but" that always follows. Saying, "This is better" implies that your child usually does poorly. It is not praise. Rather, tell your child *why* a specific behavior is good. For example, say "I like your use of adjectives in that paper. They helped me get a clear picture of what happened." This does not remind your child of past failures but does identify what can be done to create a good paper. Be specific and genuine.

You can also praise your child without words. Showing interest in what your child is doing is praise. For example, stopping to look at the picture in the book your preschooler is holding is genuine praise for his being interested in books.

Praise your child's best effort. If you wait for perfection, your child may never "merit" praise. All children need and deserve praise daily.

Don't dilute the power of praise

Your child knows when his effort is less than stellar. If you praise a sloppy job, you will reduce the power of future praise. Overused praise:

- Makes praise appear insincere;
- Increases self-focus;
- Makes a child feel that he is under constant evaluation;
- Makes a child praise-dependent.

Overused praise (i.e., praise for even the smallest thing he does correctly) makes praise appear insincere. Both you and your child know that not all of your child's behaviors deserve or need praise. If you praise him when it isn't earned, he won't believe you when you are sincere.

Overused praise increases self-focus. If your child is praised when, in reality, he needs guidance to improve his behavior or his work, he may focus only on himself. If he develops an elevated view of himself, he will not grow socially or academically. He will just assume that he can do as he pleases, and it will be praiseworthy. Egocentric and self-absorbed children rarely develop to their full potential. Praise, like food, needs to be available in helpful amounts. Under eating can lead to anorexia, and overeating will lead to obesity. Likewise, praise is essential for a healthy ego: lack of praise will lead to an anorexic ego (poor self-image), and excessive or undeserved praise will create a bloated ego (self-absorbed/exaggerated self-image).

Overused praise often makes a child feel that he is continually being evaluated and that all his behaviors are being scrutinized. If he feels his every move is being watched, he may be reluctant to try new things for fear of making a mistake. A child who does not try can never succeed! While constant evaluation reduces effort, judicial use of praise increases effort.

Overused praise can also make your child praise-dependent. Children who are praise-dependent can be manipulated by their peers and are very susceptible to bullying. On the other hand, self-praise promotes self-direction and will help your child put these bullying attempts in perspective. Starting when your child is young, you can help him reduce his reliance on praise from others and encourage him to rely on his own self-evaluations. If your child has just finished a school project, hug him and ask him what he likes best about his project. Teach your child to set standards for himself and to praise himself when he reaches his own goals. Self-praise can become a barrier against becoming praise-dependent and becoming a target for bullying.

What is too much praise? First, draw on your own experience. When have you felt that praise was being used to manipulate you? When was it insincere? Second, observe your child's reactions to your praise. Is it serving as a motivator, or making her praise-dependent? Is it helping her develop socially positive behavior, or is it making her self-focused? Praise wisely.

Encourage good decisions

SCENARIO:

In the morning, before my son-in-law left for work, he would tell my preschool grandson, "Make good decisions today."

When he returned home, he would ask, "Did you make some good decisions today?"

As they discussed the day, my son-in-law, in response to learning about good behavior, would say, "That was a good decision!"

The most common parental response to a child's good behavior is to tell the child he is a good boy. Was the innermost part of the child good or bad, or was it the decision? Which phrasing provides your child the feedback he can use in the future—"good boy" or "good decision"? Specific feedback, such as "Your *decision* kept you from getting hurt," provides guidance for future actions.

You can't always be with your child so you need to teach her to make good decisions. Start when she is young. You could ask a question like "Was it a good decision to put your milk there?" The answer probably depends on whether the milk glass was teetering on the edge of the table or placed on a level spot away from the edge. The questions will change as your child gets older. "When are you going to do your homework? Is that a good decision? Why or why not?" Discuss the consequence of the proposed decision. Motivation is an outgrowth of a belief that what happens in life is determined more by a person's decisions than by the situation.

Provide both cooperation and competition

Cooperation decreases conflict. Your family is a team. It takes everyone working together and encouraging each other for your family team to win. In sports, if team members compete to get the ball, the team will lose. If your children compete for your approval, everyone will lose. On the other hand, if you teach your children to cooperate with each other, they will do so now and as adults.

Everyone can win. To a preschool child, everyone who finishes is a winner. Being told that everyone in the class won because everyone crossed the finish line brings cheers from a group of preschoolers. If you set the timer for pick-up time and ask one of your preschoolers to pick up blocks and the other books, they will work quickly. When they both beat the timer, they will high-five you and each other. Both have won. Not so with elementary-age children. They believe only one person can be the winner. Whether this is developmental or culturally taught, it is characteristic of that age.

Competition increases focus. In the previous example, the preschoolers were focused because they were competing against the clock. Another way to use competition and still keep conflict under control is to have the child compete against himself. Your elementary child who is studying spelling words is not doing it for the joy of learning. He is doing it to pass the test—i.e., win. Rather than expecting your child to get the best grade in the class, encourage your child to do as well as, or better, than he did last week. If your child competes against himself, he has an excellent chance of winning. If only the best student wins, there will be many children who will never get to be winners. Constant losing leads to giving up. Competition has developed a bad reputation, because it is usually organized in a way that the same children always win. Having your child compete against himself can reduce this problem.

Competition can help or hurt a person. The desire to win has led some people to cheat or ignore the rights of others. A competitive drive that hasn't led to success can cause susceptibility to bullying, despair, and suicide. When you promote competition between or among your children, you will create conflict. If you always point out who has the best grades or wins the most accolades in sports, you are driving a wedge between your children. They will fight more as children and as adults.

A competitive spirit can spur a person on toward a self-chosen goal. Through the persistence that comes with a competitive spirit, many people have benefited themselves and society. Competition can help or destroy your child; it depends on how it is used. While competition can increase focus, cooperation creates a calm environment and leads to the team's success. Use both wisely.

Consider your attitude toward rules

What is your attitude toward rules? Do you view them as constraints or as a way to make life with others run more smoothly? Do you feel a need to challenge them? Do you feel a need to exert your authority and show who is boss? Your child will adopt your attitude toward rules. If you are antagonistic toward rules, your child will also be antagonistic toward rules. Since you are the nearest rule-maker, your child will decide that she should fight against your rules.

If you view the rules you have as a plan that points your child to life's winners' circle, you will probably be relaxed and confident in enforcing them. If you regard your family rules as a way to support positive family interactions, and if you explain this to your child, she will be more cooperative. Your child will mirror your attitude back to you!

Path 7

Respond Appropriately to Inappropriate Behaviors: Initial Responses

One thing is certain: despite the great techniques you learned along Paths 5 and 6 on how to reduce conflicts, problems will develop. When they do, you must respond. But how? The next three paths will answer that question.

Think Before You Act

Act like a parent

Rather than viewing your child as someone who is challenging your authority and, therefore, must be shown who is boss, view your child as someone who can benefit from your guidance and act accordingly. Keep the following in mind:

1. You have knowledge and experience that will benefit your child.
2. Your child is teachable, so teach the behaviors you want.
3. You must be calm in order to calm your child.
4. You must select responses that decrease conflict and produce the long-term results you want.
5. You must spend the energy necessary to correct his inappropriate behaviors.

6. Your responses should help your child develop appropriate behavior and self-control.

7. Your self-confidence promotes your child's confidence in your ability to control the situation.

8. You are the parent. Act like it.

Be a detective

First, determine if the situation is minor and one you can ignore. If so, relax and let it go. Pick your battles. Not every battle deserves to be fought. Excessive control results in constant fighting and actually lessens your success.

Second, before you act, determine the root of the problem:

1. Look at *yourself.* Ask, "Am I upset?" If so, calm yourself. If you can't control yourself, how do you expect to control your child? You will be more effective if you are responding calmly and intellectually.

2. Look at the *situation.* Is the situation contributing to the problem? If so, change the situation.

3. Examine your *expectations.* Ask, "Are my expectations appropriate for this situation and the developmental level of my child?" If not, adjust them so they fit the situation and your child's level of development.

4. Determine your child's *emotional state.* Ask, "Is my child's emotional state preventing a rational discussion?" If so, talk slowly and softly. Cuddle, and maybe gently restrain, your child. If your child is upset, remove him to a quiet place. You will need to calm your child before you discuss the situation with him.

5. Evaluate your child's *behavior.* Ask, "Is my child's behavior the problem?" If so, replace your child's inappropriate behavior with an appropriate behavior (see Path 8).

Answering these questions will enable you to select the best course of action.

Respond Reasonably

De-escalate, don't escalate

The scenario on Path 6, where we discussed the importance of teaching how to stop before you start, is an example of a self-reinforcing behavior that got out of hand. Out-of-control behaviors will occur, because you can't always anticipate them. You certainly don't want to escalate (increase) the problem—you will want to de-escalate (decrease) it, especially if it is self-reinforcing.

A self-reinforcing behavior is any behavior that the child continues to do because he likes it. If your child likes to practice kicking a soccer ball and therefore practices kicking a soccer ball hour after hour, kicking a soccer ball is self-reinforcing for him. If your child starts to sing "one hundred bottles of beer on the wall," you know he will continue to get louder and louder unless you intervene. He continues singing because he likes it, that is, it is self-reinforcing. Any behavior—whether it is a behavior you want or do not want—that your child continues to do because he likes it, is an example of a self-reinforcing behavior.

An escalating negative situation is any activity that gradually, or not so gradually, becomes more and more dangerous or problematic to the children involved in the activity. Just as a ball that starts rolling down a hill picks up speed, your child's out-of-control behavior will continue to pick up speed (escalate) until you stop it. De-escalate refers to slowing down the activity so it can continue without being dangerous or potentially dangerous. You are more aware of the potential dangers than the children involved in the play.

Screaming, which is a very common response, will escalate the problem, because it adds to the noise and tension. There are steps you can take to de-escalate the problem:

1. Calm yourself. Your child (or children, if you are working with a group) will pick up your emotional tone and reflect it back to you. If you scream and are angry, that is what they will reflect.
2. Go stand by your child. Being close lets you speak softly and model how you want your child to speak.
3. Calm your child. Discussing inappropriate behavior with emotionally charged child is a recipe for conflict. Don't allow yourself to be pulled into a confrontation. You may decide to rub your child's shoulders, have her sit on a chair for five minutes, or have her count to one hundred. A group could do calisthenics or a follow-the-leader sequence that gradually becomes slower. Use any parenting trick you have found useful for calming children.
4. Squat or sit in a chair so you are at your child's eye level.

5. Talk to her and the other children in a quiet voice. Calmly discuss the dangers created by their behavior. Describe the behavior you want. Establish guidelines.

6. Require all the children involved to explain or demonstrate what they will do if allowed to continue to play. Let the play resume, but stay close by.

All behavioral problems are easier to handle when they are small. Ignored, self-reinforcing problems intensify. Once in motion, your child's inappropriate behavior will stay in motion until you calmly end it by stating what he, or he and his friends, must do to continue playing.

Beware of the screaming trap

If you lose your cool and scream when your child behaves inappropriately, you will inflame the problem. Worse, your child will become "immune" to a certain noise level over time, so next time you will have to scream louder to get the same results. This will increase your parenting problems.

The appeal of screaming is understandable; it works so well initially. Your child reinforces your yelling with a quick and appropriate response. Your yelling worked; therefore, you yell the next time you want compliance. However, your child is discovering that she doesn't have to respond *until* you scream. She has time to ignore you. You conclude that your child will respond only if you yell. That is true. You taught her that! You blame your child for not responding, so you scream more frequently and louder. Screaming is an easy trap to fall into. Beware.

SCENARIO

After supper, the children were arguing over whose turn it was to load the dishwasher, wipe off the table, and put food in the refrigerator. After numerous reminders that these chores had to be done, Mom, exhausted from a highly demanding week, screamed, "Clear off this table!"

In unison, all three children and their father put silverware on their plates, lined up by the dishwasher, and quietly waited their turn to load their dishes. The four quickly cleaned up the kitchen while Mom sat there thinking, "I can certainly see why parents scream. But if I keep doing this, it will quickly lose its effectiveness, and I will have to scream louder each time. Soon they will respond only if I'm yelling at them. I don't want that to happen."

Screaming is an adult temper tantrum. Just as many adults give in to a child's temper tantrum, your child will probably give in to your adult temper tantrum. Eventually it becomes a habit, and habits are hard to break.

When you scream, you are telling your child that you are now angry enough to stop what you are doing and that you will now monitor his behavior. Why wait until you are so angry that you scream before you make certain your instructions are being followed? If you have a history of remaining calm, then a "no" with a frown will be more effective than the screams of a parent who frequently uses a loud voice. If you ignore your child and pay attention to the television until the situation gets so bad that you yell, you are teaching your child that everything is cool until you scream. Screaming indicates a loss of control. It is admitting defeat!

Signal, don't scream

It is difficult to break the habit of screaming, but you can do it by calmly replacing it with an "I've had it" signal. You may have noticed that some parents seem to get their children to obey with just a look or a slow shake of the head. You, too, can become one of those parents by learning the secret of using a signal rather than a scream. If this is new to your child, tell him you will be using a signal to let him know he must follow your rules. You can select one or more time-honored signals, such as a snap of the finger combined with a one-finger point at the offending child, counting to ten, or using your child's full name—first, middle, and last. I used all three, depending on the situation. I would then monitor my child's behavior and made certain my instructions were followed. You could teach your child that failure to respond to the signal would result in an immediate, nonverbal consequence, such as time-out or the loss of a privilege. If your child is in the habit of waiting until you scream, it will take time to teach him to respond to a calm signal. He must learn two things:

1. Not to assume he can ignore you until you scream
2. To assume you will make him comply.

If you have ever practiced a piece of music incorrectly or developed an incorrect swing in golf or baseball, you know how difficult it is to eventually learn it correctly. First you have to get rid of the poor habit. Only then can you start to learn the correct one. Likewise, your child will cling to the habit of waiting for you to scream. You will need to use your "I've had it" signal consistently and for an extended length of time before it will become effective. But, if you never use screaming and always use your "I've had it" signal, your child will learn to respond.

You will need to immediately supervise him to be certain he does what you said. You could also impose a consequence if your child does not respond to the "I've had it" signal. Your child will learn to respond without your screaming. You have now replaced a behavior you did not want (waiting until you scream) with a behavior you wanted (respond to your I've-had-it signal).

Your "I've had it" signal will lose its effectiveness if used frequently or for minor offenses. Just as the overuse of antibiotics has made them less effective over time, the overuse of your signal will cause your child to build up a tolerance and ignore it, just like he does your screaming.

Don't use your signal for daily tasks, such as picking up toys. With preschoolers, rather than screaming or using your "I've had it" signal, start the task by participating in the pick-up. With elementary-age children, give a five-minute warning that will allow them time to mentally prepare to do the task. Keep the signal for times when compliance must be immediate or is essential, such as when you feel a scream coming on, or your child's behavior is endangering himself or others. In short, you need a calm way of informing your child that you are at the end of your patience and that he must comply immediately.

If you are a new parent, don't start the screaming cycle. I guarantee there will be times when you reach your limits, and you need a way to let your child know that you are getting angry (and you *will* get angry). Having a signal will help you control both your behavior and your child's inappropriate behavior. Be a cool parent!

Signal success

Not all signals need to be firm and highly controlling, like the one discussed previously. You can also invent a signal to be a gentle reminder. You, or you and your child, can select a behavior that she will work on, along with a secret signal you can use to remind her to modify the selected behavior.

First, select the one rule or task you will work on initially. Second, you and your child will select a secret signal to be used as a reminder when she forgets her target rule or task. The signal says, "Cool it; think about what you are doing." You and your child can come up with your own signal or select one of the following:

- Shaking your head slowly
- Putting your finger on your cheek or ear
- Crossing your arms in front of you

Keeping with the theme of having a special secret, you should use a signal to show approval or praise. When your child responds appropriately, she should receive a wink or thumbs-up to let her know you are proud of her behavior. When you use this approach, you are changing a corrective action into a game. Children who love games respond well to this approach. This approach may not be controlling enough for the hard-to-control child.

This approach works well for the parent who is trying to help a child develop a habit that requires frequent reminders. Using a signal has several advantages. It allows you to correct the behavior without calling attention to the behavior in public or having a verbal confrontation. It may also reduce the anger you feel over constantly correcting a specific behavior.

It is best to work on one behavior at a time. Once that behavior is established, pick a new focus and work on it. Once a behavior is established, it can be maintained with periodic secret-signal reminders.

Respond immediately

Just as consistency is the most important factor in reducing future problems, the immediacy of your response is the most important factor when responding to an inappropriate behavior. A response or consequence does not need to be severe or long, but it does need to be administered immediately. There are several reasons for this.

A response is *more powerful* if it is given immediately than if it is delayed. We see this in many areas of life. For example, people often overindulge in alcohol despite knowing they will have a dreadful, painful hangover the next day. The immediate pleasurable feeling they get from drinking is strong while the hangover doesn't come until the next morning, thus reducing its negative impact. If your response to inappropriate behavior is delayed, your impact on your child's behavior is diminished. A consequence given at a later time can change a behavior, but to do so, it must be more intense than if given immediately. Your delayed, intense response will be an unhappy experience for both you and your child. If you respond immediately, your calm, firm response will be effective.

Immediacy is powerful because people *associate (connect)* events that happen in proximity (in space or time) of each other. Companies incorporate smiling people into their advertisements, because they want to immediately link joy with their product. Seeing a smiling person and the car together connects "pleasure" and "car." Likewise, if your child experiences the misbehavior and the consequence in the same time span, the two events become linked.

When (not *if*) your child misbehaves in public, get down to the child's eye level, hold his face in your hand so he faces you and sees the displeasure on your face, and state clearly what he must do. This will have more impact than yelling later or sending him to his room for two hours when you get home.

Delaying your response or waiting for the absent parent to discipline your child later will reduce the power of the consequence. Thus, the severity of the consequence will need to be increased if it is going to have any effect. Also, your child will conclude that only the disciplining parent must be obeyed. The parent who is present at the time of the inappropriate behavior needs to intervene and know that the child's other parent will support the decision. This is just one of the reasons parents need a unified approach to parenting.

Don't call a fire truck to put out a candle

It is so easy to conclude that if your initial response is firm enough, the problem will go away once and for all. In reality, your initial response is just the baseline on which to build future corrective actions. Therefore, the severity of your response must be appropriate for the severity of the misbehavior. If your response to a minor infraction of a rule is a major consequence, what will you do for an encore when your child's behavior is more damaging to herself or others? You need to save the most severe reactions for the most severe problems. Over reacting would be akin to calling the fire truck to put out a candle.

SCENARIO

School is out for the summer. Three brothers, in a mood to celebrate, made a noisy entrance through their front door. They shoved and high-fived each other, loudly pronouncing, "School's out!"

Mother, exhausted just thinking about the long summer ahead, screamed, "Quiet! Quiet, I said!" Yelling, wrestling, and fighting continued. Mother yelled, "Sit in that chair. You almost knocked the lamp over." The boys, in their exuberance, ignored her, and the noise and activity escalated. Mom walked angrily toward them and announced, "Quiet down, or I will ground you for the entire summer." There was still no change in the boys' behavior. "That's it!" she screamed. "You are grounded for the entire summer!"

This poor mother suffered all summer with her three boys grounded to the backyard. She probably felt that, in order to be consistent, she needed to carry out her threat. In reality, she was being rigid. Basically, she punished herself for overreacting.

The boys enjoyed their interactions (the wrestling was self-reinforcing), and each encouraged the other to become more and more rowdy, thus escalating the problem. Ideally the mother would have anticipated their exuberance and been prepared. Since she needed to intervene, she could have modeled calm behavior and in a quiet voice assured them she understood the excitement they felt knowing school was out. She could have provided a quiet way to celebrate, such as offering them a sit-down treat or she could have sent them to different areas of the house, so they wouldn't stimulate each other. The nature of the offense—excessive excitement due to an identifiable event—required a calming response, not an extreme punishment.

Once she blurted out the consequence, she still had a chance to turn it into a learning experience. They could have discussed the importance of family members helping each other and the reality that all people—including parents—make mistakes. Believe me, your child already knows you make mistakes. She could have taken responsibility for her mistake and modeled how to correct one's mistakes. Together they could decide on a consequence appropriate for the severity of the problem. Modeling is a great teacher.

Your response to inappropriate behavior should not only fit the severity of the problem but should move your child toward the behavior you want. For example, if your child fails a test, have him review that information. Since he failed to schedule enough study time to pass the test, you get to schedule the length, time, and location of the next study session. Don't make it so long that there is time for nothing else. It could be fifteen minutes each day for the rest of the week. If the grade does not improve, add specific tasks that the teacher recommends. This limited response is more effective than removing all sports or recreational time until the next report card comes out. When the hope for relief is so far away, your child loses hope and reduces his effort. When you focus on the behavior you want, your response will not be to punish but rather to help your child achieve the desired behaviors.

If your child's behavior is self-destructive or harmful to others, you need to react firmly. Yes, there are times to call the fire truck but not to put out a candle.

Know when to say "no"

As you learned on Path 4, toddlers are infamous for their use of "no." You were advised to ignore her "no" and to use "no" infrequently. The word "no" can definitely be overused. I like to think of each baby arriving at her home with a bag of "no's" to be given out judiciously. If they are given frequently and unnecessarily, they will all be used up in a short time. Then there will be none available when they are really needed. A judiciously used "no" works, therefore, you need to know when and how to use them. Rather than respond with an automatic "no," gather information about the situation. This enables you to make a better decision, which prevents you from having to decide whether to enforce a poor decision or to change it. Gathering information, such as the type of questions to ask prior to making a decision, models good decision-making skills. It also enables you to explain the reason for your decision and how it relates to your rules and values. This leads to your child internalizing your values and promotes her self-control.

Some parenting books advise against using "no" entirely for the following reasons:

- "No" tells your child what *not* to do but does not tell her what she should do.
- "No," if overused, loses its impact.
- "No" creates a negative tone in the home.

Telling your child what you want her to do is more effective than saying "no." While an overused "no" is very ineffective, a judiciously used "no" can work.

Praise in public; correct in private

When a child does something praiseworthy, praise him in front of the other children. If he breaks rules and you need to correct him, take the offending child to the side and correct him out of the sight of other children. Whether you are praising or correcting a behavior in the presence of other children you are calling attention to that behavior, so use this as an opportunity to call attention only to the behaviors you want. Other children will try that behavior, because children do what is modeled. That behavior will be reinforced by the attention received from the adult *and* from siblings and peers. You want to encourage siblings and others to notice the good behavior and join in the praise. Therefore, praise in public.

Children throughout the ages have been intrigued by rebellious or naughty behavior. Many a toddler has thrown a temper tantrum like the one he observed, even when the offending child was punished. The elementary-age child focuses on friendships and may get great pleasure showing siblings and peers that he can take the punishment you dish out. Standing up to an adult often brings the elementary-age child the adulation of peers. Think back to your childhood or to the books you read as a child. There is always the child who bravely stood up to the adult and didn't wince when punished—an indication of great bravery. I can almost hear some parent saying, "My child won't feel brave when I get through with him!" To that parent, I say, "Why raise your blood pressure by angrily confronting your child when having your child face you without support from observers makes a calm response effective?" A child receiving or observing a scolding may view it differently from the adult administering the scolding. The adult views it as a warning against repeating the behavior. Your child may view it as attention or a way to show defiance.

When it comes to reacting to adult correction in public, children seem to divide into two groups—defiant or crushed. Public criticism can become part of your child's self-image of "being bad." On the other hand, a child who tends to be defiant can use this to prove that he is big and tough. Both reactions are counterproductive. Correction, given in private, removes your child from the embarrassing or reinforcing attention of siblings and peers. There are many advantages to praising your child in front of peers, but there are no advantages to correcting him in front them.

Path 8

Respond Appropriately to Inappropriate Behaviors: Controlling Responses

There are times when your child dares you to make him follow your instructions. On those occasions, you need to be firm and maximize your parental control. You must also act firmly and quickly when safety requires immediate obedience. When a decision requires knowledge and maturity your child lacks, you must make the decision for him. This Path will teach you ways to do that.

What Will You Do if I Won't?

Ignore attention-getting behaviors

Planned ignoring is not a passive response to your child's actions. Rather, it is a highly controlled approach to inappropriate behaviors that a child will use to get her way. Since her misbehavior probably angers or embarrasses you, your first reaction may be to respond strongly. Ignoring her behavior will require you to exercise a great deal of self-control.

Warning: When appropriate, ignoring is a good and highly controlling approach, but it is *not* always appropriate. Never ignore a behavior:

- That could endanger your children or another child;
- Because you are busy or just don't want to be bothered at that time;
- That enables your children to get what they want (self-reinforcing).

Don't ignore any of those behaviors! Step in immediately and, in positive terms, tell your child exactly what you want him to do.

When to use: Do *plan* to ignore behaviors that your child is using to manipulate you, such as whining, temper tantrums, and her persistent use of the word "no." If you ignore the tantrums (I know that is hard to do), and your child does not receive what she wants, her bad behaviors will decrease. Really, they will! If safety permits, turn away from your child or walk out of the room. Your presence gives her the hope that she can win if she just screams long enough and loud enough.

Persist. Once you decide to ignore a behavior, you must continue to ignore it until the behavior stops. Inappropriate behaviors that work part of the time but not all the time are the hardest to eliminate. If you ignore tantrums most of the time but occasionally give in, you are actually encouraging your child to keep throwing tantrums for longer times. She remembers that one time when you gave in and concludes that there still is hope she can win if she only tries long and hard enough. In those cases, the tantrums will increase in intensity and frequency.

Avoid inconsistency. Ignoring your child's behavior because you are exhausted or distracted by other events is *not* planned ignoring. If ignoring a behavior enables your child to get by with something that is against your rules, he will continue to do it. This inconsistency will make parenting difficult.

Be deliberate. This technique is based on the psychological principle that people do what works but stop doing things that do not work. Planned ignoring is your *deliberate* decision not to pay attention to your child's behavior, because he is using this behavior to get your attention or to manipulate you. If you give in to him, you are letting your child control your behavior.

Dealing with your resourceful child. Your child is wise! He knows that screaming louder is not the only way to increase the probability that his temper tantrum will work. He can do that simply by throwing a tantrum in a public place like the grocery store. Ideally, you can ignore his behavior. Of course, you must stay where you can see that he is not harming himself or destroying the store. If you find that you cannot ignore this behavior, you may need to leave the store immediately— without treats, eating out, or playtime in the car or at home. Isolate your child in his room, only permitting him to come out when he stops yelling. Do not lecture him or provide verbal interaction at this time. This is not the time to discuss proper behavior. A child throwing a temper tantrum will not listen to reason. This is the time to control your child by removing all attention.

An ounce of prevention accomplishes more than a pound of cure. Prevention is always the best approach to dealing with tantrums. Avoid tantrum-producing activities, such as shopping when your child is tired or hungry. Keep trips short. As I mentioned before, the time to discuss what happened at the store is not when you return from the store but rather before your next trip to the store. When you are getting ready for your next trip, remind your child of the rules and the consequences she experienced on the previous trip to the store. Rather than telling her what she must not do (e.g., don't yell and demand cookies), tell her what she must do (e.g., hold on to the cart at all times). Tell her that if she uses a quiet, pleasant voice, she may select one item (e.g., a type of cookie). Give her something to do at the store. You can give her a shopping list to fill, including an item of her choosing. Hopefully there is something on the list she wants badly enough that she will cooperate. If she starts to yell, leave immediately. Repeat the no-verbal-interaction, no-treats, and isolation scenario. The trick is to stay calm longer than she can throw tantrums. The contest to determine which of you has more self-control has started. Don't give in. I'm rooting for you! This scenario will repeat itself; however, your child will eventually stop the inappropriate behavior if she does not get what she wants.

Avoid psychological judo

Your child is a good psychologist. He hasn't read any books on psychology and may not even be able to say the word, but he knows how to use the principles of psychology to get what he wants. If you give in so he will stop whining, your child will "reinforce you" by stopping his whining. Your child knows that you don't like his screaming and crying, so if you give in, he stops. Reinforcers work. If you like the quiet that follows, you will probably give in to him the next time. When you give in, you are using the power of the reinforcer against yourself. That is what I call psychological judo.

In judo, your opponent uses your attempt to lessen your pain (e.g., stop the crying) and your own strength (i.e., being the decision maker) to defeat you. In Judo, your opponent can twist your arm behind your back, thus inflicting pain. Your natural reaction is to reduce the pain by moving in the direction of the twisted arm allowing your opponent to flip you. This approach enables a smaller, less-powerful person to control a larger, stronger person. If your child uses crying and screaming to get her way, your natural reaction may be to stop this behavior (i.e., reduce your pain) by giving in. Yes, you will stop the momentary pain, but you are also causing your own fall. Thus a smaller, less-powerful person (your child) can control the behavior of a stronger person (you).

Make certain your response is age-appropriate. Responding to your infant's cry for food or comfort, which is her only way to communicate, is teaching her to trust you. On the other hand, giving in to your toddler's kicking and screaming is an example of psychological judo. Avoid psychological judo.

Reduce conflict with time-out

If your child is using inappropriate behavior to get your attention, you can use planned ignoring. If an *activity or situation* is contributing to the behavior you do not want, you can remove your child from that activity or situation and use time-out. Time-out, which is very explicit and standard in its application, is extremely valuable with some children. For example, if a child:

• Has limited verbal understanding due to age or ability, using time-out provides you with a technique where language is less important;

• Has limited self-control because of age, temperament, or a special need, this approach will provide the structure you need;

• Has an ingrained inappropriate behavior, this approach can provide clear boundaries;

• Constantly questions your rules, this approach lets you enforce these rules without getting pulled into an argument.

Use few or no words. "Time-out" is a shorthand way to say "time-out from reinforcers" and is based on the principle that behaviors that do not work will stop. For example, time-out is effective when the situation is overly stimulating and contributes to your child's aggressive or loud behavior. He may hit a playmate to get a toy. He wants to remain in the play setting, but you remove him from this "exciting" (reinforcing) activity. Since the goal is to remove your child from any reinforcers, use few or no words as all talking, including scolding, can be reinforcing. Keep your interactions to a minimum. Time-out must be applied automatically and without an emotional outburst from you. Whining, pleading, bargaining, hitting or any other response must be ignored. Say, "Go to the time-out chair" or use a previously taught hand signal, such as snapping your fingers and pointing to the chair. Use a timer to keep the time. If your child leaves the chair before the required time, the timer is restarted without any scolding from you.

Control your child's access to what he wants. Your child should be placed where he will not get attention but can observe the activity or people he would like to rejoin. Once he regains self-control, he may reenter the play situation. The delight and pleasure he experiences when he returns to the activity are internal reinforcers and, therefore, more powerful than external reinforcers like candy. When you permit your child to return, the play situation becomes the reinforcer.

Each time-out should be brief, about one minute for each year of the preschool child's age. Five minutes should be adequate for the elementary-age child. When the required time is up, tell your child that he can return to his previous activity. If he does not behave when he returns, you need to use your hand signal, restart the timer, and send him back to time-out. Successful time-outs require you to use few to no words, to remain calm, and always to follow the same procedure.

Modify time-out. Be creative. You can vary time-out to fit your family's interests. The following example shows how a family made time-out function smoothly in their home.

SCENARIO

The parents in a family of avid soccer fans used yellow and red cards to signal "penalties," just as you would in a soccer game. When a child started to get too rowdy, he would get a yellow card. If the child received two yellow cards, he would have to "sit on the bench." If the parent judged the offense warranted a red card, they would give him a red card. When they displayed a red card, the boy slumped and said, "Oh, man," and shuffled off to the "bench."

I applaud these parents for coming up with a family-appropriate variation of a common intervention. They maintained the fundamental characteristics of time-out—immediate removal from a desired activity with few or no words. I want to encourage you to take this basic concept, learn how it works, and adapt it to your family's needs.

Count your way to success

My second example of successfully adapting time-out melds the time-honored approach of counting to ten and the presently popular method of time-out. When your parents started to count to ten, you probably knew you had better behave. Counting lets your child know how much time she has to gain control of herself before being sent to the time-out chair.

In his book *1-2-3 Magic*, Dr. Phelan advises parents to add counting and a brief explanation of the child's inappropriate behavior. Tell your child what you expect and explain it only one time. If your child does not comply, you count as described below:

- Say "One." You must be quiet and give no response to the child's words or actions. If your child complies, stop counting. If he does not comply, continue counting.
- Say "Two." Continue to remain quiet. If your child complies, stop counting. If not, continue counting.
- Say "Three; take five." At this point, your child should be sent to his room or a chair for five minutes.

When you send your child to his room, there should be no discussion. No phone, no friends, no television, and no computer games are permitted. This approach permits napping, listening to the radio, playing with toys, and similar activities. It also advises the parent that if the child wrecks his room, they should leave it alone and let him live in the mess. The child must learn the meaning behind counting, and it should be used without variation if it is going to be successful.

Know the limitations of time-out

There are situations where time-out won't work. Time-out is ineffective if your child misbehaves because she is bored. It lets her escape a boring situation, and, in these cases, removing her and sending her to sit in a chair may actually reinforce her behavior. For example, if your child misbehaves while waiting for others to finish eating, she may find time-out to be a diversion from the boredom of sitting at the table. Also, time-out does not work as a delayed consequence. For example, if your child misbehaves in the doctor's waiting room or at the store, warning her to be quiet or else you will send her to the time-out chair when you get home will not be a deterrent. On the other hand, a thinking chair (discussed on Path 9) can be used.

All these variations of time-out enable the parent to remain in control. Since this technique uses few words, there is less opportunity for a child-parent conflict. Therefore, time-out is extremely useful to parents who find that they get angry when disciplining.

Critics of this controlling parenting technique claim it develops a dependency on external control of behavior. Most people, at least on some occasions, modify their actions based on external control. If you have ever adjusted your driving speed because you spotted a police car, then you too have responded to an external control. Or if taxes were collected only on an honor basis, I doubt if our government would get much money. Therefore, I am comfortable including a technique that relies on external controls as *one* of the many ways to parent.

Time-out, and the other highly controlling techniques discussed previously, will train your child to obey, but they do not help her develop either self-control or concern for others. They also do not teach your child how to analyze social situations so she can avoid future conflicts. To develop those characteristics, you will need to add the techniques discussed on Path 9.

Remove a misused privilege

Having friends over, watching TV, having a cell phone, doing activities on a computer or technology device, and many other things your child regards as his right, are, in reality, privileges. If misused, these privileges should be removed. In fact, you can remove any of these privileges as a consequence for not adhering to your rules.

Consequences should be explained calmly and firmly. The privilege lost should:

- be one your children value;
- be similar to the offending behavior;
- reflect the seriousness of the offense in duration and severity;
- be administered immediately.

SCENARIO
Matt: What will you do if I don't?
Mom: That's the wrong question. It implies you have the option of not doing what you are told, and that is not an option. The question is, how many privileges will you lose before you obey? I will find something you want badly enough that you will do this. The first consequence will be a minor one to let you know I mean business. If you obey me then, you will have lost very little. If you persist, the consequences will increase. Are you going to comply now or after you have lost privileges?
Matt complied prior to losing any privileges.

The threat of a consequence was all that Matt needed because Mom had followed through in the past. She limited the consequences to what was absolutely necessary for that situation. The goal was not to punish him but to make certain that he followed her rules.

Impose grounding

Grounding your child—that is, requiring him to spend time at home or in his room—is a time-honored parenting technique. Parents frequently complain that the effort it takes to enforce grounding their child makes them feel as if they are being punished more than the child. But when your child goes to a forbidden place or doesn't make it home by the required time, grounding him may be the punishment most directly related to the rule infraction.

To be effective, grounding requires you to control access to what your child wants. She may have so many fascinating technological toys—televisions, computers, iPods, and other devices—that doing time in her room is like being sent to Disneyland. This may make the guest room, laundry room, dining room, or another room more suitable than her bedroom as the required place to stay. Permit your child to do homework or tasks that will help the family, such as folding laundry.

Grounding your child immediately is more important than how long you ground your child. A first offense may warrant being grounded for an hour or less. When the first grounding has ended, explain that the length of the punishment will be increased with each repeated offense. If there is a second offense, ground her for a longer time. The goal is to show your child that you will carry out your grounding plan. At the end of the second offense, ask her how long she was grounded the first time. Ask her if the consequence was what she had been told it would be. Hopefully, it was. Tell her how much longer she will be grounded if there is a third offense. Remind your child that, as in the past, you will continue to enforce your rules in the future.

A word to the wise: If you are calm and consistent, this approach will reduce conflicts and decrease inappropriate behaviors. But if you lose your cool, you will focus her attention on you and not on her inappropriate behavior. If you do not always (and I do mean *always*) follow through, you will have created more problems, and your child's inappropriate behavior will become harder and harder to control.

Replace an Inappropriate Behavior with an Appropriate Behavior

On Path 5 I explained how to replace inappropriate communication, such as whining and crying, with appropriate communication, such as words. You did not let your child get what he wanted by whining and crying (i.e., you stopped reinforcing his inappropriate behavior), and you required words (i.e., you reinforced the desired behavior). This approach was used again on Path 7 where you learned how to replace your child's behavior of waiting until you screamed with the behavior of responding to your "I've-had-it" signal. In these two situations, you replaced an inappropriate behavior with an appropriate behavior in just two steps. While all replacement approaches require those two steps, some behaviors, such as the two explained below, are complex and may require you to spend weeks, months, and even years establishing the desired behaviors. It is my hope that learning how to replace an inappropriate behavior with one you want using only two steps will make it easier to understand how to achieve the same goal when multiple steps are needed.

Step up to success

It is easy to get to the second floor of your home because there are small steps that you can take to get there. Likewise, if you provide small, achievable steps that lead to the behavior you want, your child will be successful. Learning occurs gradually, so be patient.

Select one behavior you want to change. Work on replacing just one inappropriate behavior at a time. If this parenting approach is new to you, try practicing it in an easier format before applying it to more complex problem areas. I will provide you an overview of the process and then walk you through two examples. I will use a sport skill for my first example, because the behaviors are observable, and you may have previously seen or used this general approach to teach a sport skill. The second example will be an inappropriate behavior that is replaced with an appropriate behavior.

Removing your child's inappropriate behavior and replacing it with an appropriate behavior can be done in the following small steps:

1. Select the behavior you want to replace.
2. Don't let the inappropriate behavior work (i.e., stop reinforcing it).
3. Select the target behavior (i.e., the final, desired behavior).
4. Select the reward for doing the target (desired) behavior.
5. Determine, by observing your child, what he can do at this time.
6. Plan small, sequential steps that will gradually lead to the targeted behavior:
   - Your child must be successfully doing the task before going on to the next level.
   - Continue to gradually increase your expectations until he can successfully perform the desired end behavior.
7. Decrease the frequency of giving the reward until it is rarely or never given.

Replace not hitting the ball with hitting a pitched ball. I selected teaching this sport skill as my first example as I think you may be familiar with the gradual way baseball is taught. The following example of teaching a child to bat demonstrates how the skill of batting can be introduced using the previously listed steps:

1. *Select the behavior that you want to replace.* The behavior you want to replace or eliminate is missing the ball when he swings the bat.

2. *Don't let the inappropriate behavior work.* Reduce the likelihood that your child will miss hitting the ball with the bat by simplifying the task (see sequential steps listed below).

3. *Select the target behavior.* The target behavior is to swing the bat and hit a pitched ball.

4. *Select a reward.* The reward is hitting the ball. Success is the most powerful of all the reinforcers.

5. *Determine, by observing your child, what he can do at this time.* At this time, your child can hold the bat somewhat straight and still.

6. *Plan small, sequential steps to teach the target behavior.* Be sure that your child can successfully do task A before going to task B and that he can do task B before going to task C. Always assure success before you go to the next step.

   A. Place the ball on a stable stand and have him swing at the ball.

   B. Place the ball on a hanging rope and have him swing at it. Stay at this level until your child consistently can hit the hanging ball.

   C. Gently swing the ball and have your child bat the moving ball. Continue at this level until your child can successfully hit the ball 80 percent of the time.

D. You pitch to your child; you aim at the bat.

E. You vary your pitches slightly.

F. He will progress from T-ball to parent-pitched ball to peer-pitched ball. Your child may even progress to playing high school or college ball.

7. Decrease the frequency of giving instructions.

Apply your new skill

You learned how to increase a sport skill using small steps. Now I will explain how you can use small steps to get rid of an inappropriate behavior (e.g., scattering school books and papers throughout your home) and replace it with one you want (e.g., putting everything where it belongs). We will use the same seven steps listed earlier to create our plan:

1. *Select the behavior that you want to replace.* We will eliminate your child's habit of dropping her coat, books, and papers in various places throughout the house when she returns from school.

2. *Don't let her inappropriate behavior work.* Do not permit her to play or eat until she has put her school items where they belong.

3. *Select the target behavior.* You want your child to place her school items where they will be accessible for doing homework and findable the next day. You want her to show you her schoolwork. You show her where each item should be stored.

4. *Select a reward* that your child will like. Since she has been in a controlled environment at school, she probably wants the freedom to play. She is probably hungry. Let her eat a healthy snack and go play after she puts everything where it belongs. The reward must be something she likes and wants.

5. *Determine what she is capable of doing at this time.* You are not asking yourself what children of this age can or should do. You are looking only at *your child and what she can actually do.* For this example, we are saying that the parent, after observing her child, has determined that the child has the skills needed to put the school items away but does not put them away. Therefore, the parent will require the complete target behavior from the

beginning but will provide reminders and assistance throughout the task.

6. *Plan small, sequential steps* that will gradually lead to the target behavior. Do the tasks in the same order each day. Always start by giving the instruction that encompasses the entire task, which, in this case, is "Put all your school items where they belong." For this example I have decided to include four tasks. I started with "Hang up your coat" and ended with "Put your backpack next to the door." Walk your child through the task:

- "Put all your school items where they belong" (i.e., the general, overarching instruction which you will give throughout the learning process).
- "Hang up your coat." Show the location and supervise.
- "Show me your schoolwork and notices." Stop and look at them.
- "Organize your homework assignments and place them here." Set up to do homework later. Supervise the setup.
- "Put your backpack next to the door so it will be ready to go back to school." Watch to make certain it is done. This is the first task you will stop supervising.

7. Initially, do all the steps with her and give her verbal reminders for each step. Always start the process using the same words. You will stop helping or supervising starting with the *last task* (in this case, "Put your backpack next to door so it will be ready to go back to school.") When you think she will probably remember to do this last task without a reminder, walk away and let her complete it without supervision. By not helping her do the last step, you are teaching her to complete the task on her own and promoting a feeling of success.

The next day you will start by giving the general instruction and then assisting with each of the first tasks but, if you see that she is starting to put the backpack away without a reminder, step away and let her do the task without a reminder. Once she consistently and without a reminder or assistance does the last task of putting the backpack where it belongs, watch to see if she starts, without being reminded, to do the next to last step, "Organize your homework assignments and place them here." When your child no longer needs a reminder to place the last two items (backpack and homework) where they belong, drop those reminders. Continue eliminating reminders, starting with the last one and continuing up the list until all you need to say is "Put everything where it belongs," and she completes all four tasks without assistance. Give reminders and assistance as long as needed, but only as long as needed.

Continue to give the overarching reminder, until the simple act of walking in the door reminds her to put everything where it belongs. Once this happens, you have successfully replaced a behavior you did not want (i.e., dropping her books, papers, and coat in various places throughout the house when she returns from school) with the habit you do want (i.e., putting everything where it belongs). Be pleasant and upbeat as you model each step. Make your time together enjoyable. Your child misses you when she is in school and will benefit from this time with you.

There are three key factors you must remember when replacing an inappropriate behavior with an appropriate behavior. The first and most important factor is to *ensure her success at each level.* You must start with a behavior she can perform easily and increase your expectations gradually. Second, always start with a *reminder that encompasses the entire task* and then start the tasks with her. Third, provide *assistance and reminders* as needed, but don't continue them beyond the time needed.

I can almost hear you saying, "That's too slow. I'll just demand that the items are put away. No need to do it in small steps." Yes, you can nag and yell at her. She may eventually learn to put her things away, but you are developing an interaction pattern where you scream and get irritated and she balks. This is not a pattern you want. A calm approach will get you the results you want more quickly and create a positive parent-child interaction pattern that will make future parenting enjoyable.

This powerful approach has broad applications. If your child has a behavior you want to stop and *you know what behavior you want instead of the inappropriate behavior*, you can use this approach. The key is to know what behavior you want. You will be successful if you break the task into small steps and are willing to be calm and to proceed slowly. It can be used with a young toddler or a child of any age. If you have a hard-to-control child or a special-needs child, learning this approach is a must. In no time at all, seeing how to simplify a task and how to break it into its parts will become second nature to you, and you will find using it easy and rewarding.

We've come to the end of Path 8, where you have learned some controlling, yet appropriate, responses to your child's inappropriate behaviors.

Path 9

Develop Your Child's Self-Control

On this path we will explore ways to develop your child's ability to and interest in maintaining your values and your rules even when your are not there to guide him.

Provide Choices within Limits

Increase your child's options

The freedom-within-limits approaches we will discuss on this path will enable your child to become a self-regulated person by gradually increasing his input:

- They require your child to take responsibility for his actions.
- They develop problem-solving skills.
- They promote self-control.

To achieve these goals, you must give up some of your control. If you are highly controlling in other areas of your life, you may find this difficult. On the other hand, if you enjoy the give-and-take of a discussion and regard a range of behaviors as acceptable, then you will enjoy using these open-ended approaches.

You must provide boundaries that are appropriate for the age and temperament of your child. You cannot always be with your child; therefore, you must teach values and problem-solving skills that your child can use when making his own decisions.

Don't sweat the small stuff

Are your child's unwanted behaviors ones with long-range implications, or do you disagree on small things that are unimportant in the long run? If you are like most parents, you spend a great deal of energy fighting with your child over minor issues. Relax! Let her make decisions that relate to her daily life, such as cleaning her room, food choices, hairstyles, and clothing. If you don't sweat the small stuff and let her experience the natural consequences of her decisions, you are providing opportunities for her to see the relationship between her decisions and their consequences.

A common area of conflict is the child's messy room. Don't worry if her room isn't picked up. Unless the local philanthropic group has placed your home on a fundraising tour, just close the door. I know you wonder how anyone could live in such a mess. She can, so relax.

Maybe your child didn't get all her fruits and vegetables today. Remember, there is always tomorrow. You can set the food limits by buying only the foods you regard as appropriate. Let her select from what you buy. If donuts are not in the house, they are not a possible choice for breakfast. However, if you feel your child is showing behaviors that may point to a more serious condition such as anorexia and/or bulimia you should seek professional help for your child.

Don't let your child's choice of hairstyles raise your blood pressure. Your limits need to be broad enough to allow your child to try out "new" styles. This hairstyle will pass. Your child will grow up and choose more appropriate hairstyles.

Your child should start making decisions within guidelines at an early age. Letting your child select the clothes she will wear is an easy place to start. When getting out the clothes to wear to preschool the next day, let your child choose which of two tops to wear. When she is in kindergarten, put school clothes in a specific part of the closet and in specific drawers. Let her pick out her entire school outfit from those areas. Don't worry if they don't "match" or if her choices don't meet your standards. Every generation develops its own fashion style. You may be as bewildered by your preteen's choices as your parents were about yours. As long as it meets school guidelines and basic social decency guidelines (which a parent has every right to set), the choice is hers.

On the other hand, if your preteen's hairstyle or clothing choices indicate membership in a rebellious or antisocial group, then you need to determine what your child is getting from associating with that group. Acceptance? Where else can she get that acceptance? Rather than fight with her over her choice of hairstyle or clothing, deal with the needs she is expressing.

Please note that these examples included safe, age-appropriate boundaries that left space for your child to make decisions. You need to trust your child and accept the fact that he will make choices that you may not like. You make mistakes, and so will he. But, if he abuses this freedom, you should take away some of his decision-making privileges. Yes, I did call them privileges. After a discussion about what went wrong, return the privileges.

How can you get your child to the point where she will make decisions that will benefit her and others? By letting her make little decisions when she is little and bigger decisions when she is bigger. You can do this if you remember not to sweat the small stuff.

Promote Your Child's Thinking

Rather than just correcting your child's inappropriate behaviors, encourage your child to reflect on them. We will explore how experiencing the natural consequences of his behavior, skillful questioning, and being sent to a thinking chair will teach him how to evaluate his own behavior. Using his self-evaluation he will be able to create his own plan for controlling and changing his behavior.

Provide a dose of reality

The real world can be an effective, though sometimes harsh, teacher. A natural consequence removes you as an arbitrary dispenser of consequences and is a valuable teaching tool. It encourages your child to take responsibility for her actions as well as increase her awareness that she can cause things to happen (i.e., she is a causal agent). In addition, it encourages your child to think about her actions and allows her to monitor her own behavior.

While this approach cannot be used if it endangers your child or others, it can be highly effective in many situations. For example, when the bike he forgot to put away is run over by a car, he is more likely to understand why he should have put it away if he is now responsible for replacing it. Don't soften the impact of the natural consequence by offering to fix it or buy a new one! He can ride the scratched bike or if it is too damaged, he can earn money to have it repaired.

If your child connects his behavior to what happened, silence is golden. Giving him a lecture will enable him to divide his attention between the consequence of his actions and the discomfort he feels when you are scolding him. If, on the other hand, he seems oblivious to his role in what happened, ask him very matter-of-fact questions such as, "How did this happen?" Questions that enable him to see the connection between what he did and what happened are more powerful than pointing out the connection or scolding him.

While you must assure safety, you can also let the natural consequence be her teacher. Relax. Take a deep breath, and be grateful that you don't always have to be the bad guy. Let the big bad world do it for you.

Stimulate thinking by using questions

Questioning your child, although not a new parenting technique, is rarely used to its full advantage. Questioning can just as easily escalate conflict as it can solve it. You need to know the various types of questions and how to use them effectively. Questions can:

- Stimulate thinking (open-ended questions) or limit thinking (closed-end questions);
- Interrogate;
- Focus your children's attention on various aspects of the problem, which will promote problem-solving skills;
- Teach your values when you ask questions that connect a specific situation to your value system.

SCENARIO

Ryan, a third grader, was agitated when he came home from school. He complained, "The school bus driver told me to sit down and be quiet, or she was going to give me a pink slip."

Mom: Whom were you talking to?

Ryan: The bus driver.

Mom: Tell me about it.

Ryan: Well, yesterday, I told her that she should move the bus stop from the corner to the middle of the block. At the corner, we don't have a place to get out of the rain, but in the middle of the block, we can wait under our carport when it's raining.

Mom: What did she say?

Ryan: Sit down.

Mom: Did you?

Ryan: Yes. Then this morning I told her I asked everyone who gets on here if they would rather have the stop at the corner or in the middle of the block. She told me to sit down. I told her that six people wanted to move it to the middle of the block and only two wanted it at the corner. Before I could finish, she said, "Sit down." Then I told her I counted the number of houses each of us had to pass and added them together. I told her the total number of houses we passed if we met in the middle of the block and if we all had to walk to the end. Since only two people would have to walk past more houses and six people would walk past a lot less, there would be less total walking if the bus stop were in the middle of the block.

Mom: What did she say?

Ryan: Sit down and be quiet, or I'll give you a pink slip.

Mom: Do you think that conversation would be okay to have at home?

Ryan: Yes, because I was just explaining a better way to do it.

Mom: Right. You did a lot of thinking and we encourage that. But now I want you to think how the job of a parent and the job of a bus driver are different. What is the job of a bus driver?
Ryan: To drive us to school and get us there safely and on time.
Mom: Does talking to you help her do her job?
Ryan: No.
Mother: Why do you think she threaten you with a pink slip?
Ryan: Talking distracted her from driving and she needed to drive safely.
Mom: So some things that work at home don't work other places. You thought it through very carefully and made very good points but, the school and the bus company, not the driver, decides where the buses will stop. What do you plan to do now?
Ryan: Let her do her job.

The previous scenario used open-ended questions to stimulate thinking and closed-ended questions to get specific information. Asking Ryan open-ended questions promoted thinking and encouraged him to tell the entire story. For example, when the parent asked the open-ended question, "Tell me about it" she was encouraging Ryan to present his view. She did active listening, refrained from evaluating his actions, and asked questions that promoted continued discussion. Only after he had completed the story did she ask him to evaluate what had happened. At that point, she asked him to contrast his parents' job with the bus driver's job. This required him to think beyond the specifics of the incident and to incorporate insights he had obtained from previous experiences with his parents and the bus driver. Next he had to apply them to this specific situation.

Closed-ended questions have one correct answer and, therefore, imply you expect him to come up with that answer. If, in the early stage of the discussion, Ryan had been asked a yes or no question such as, "Since the bus driver told you 'no,' don't you think you should have stopped asking?" He probably would have concluded that his mother was critical of his actions and, therefore, he wouldn't have continued to share his experience. When a child feels he needs to give you the "right" answer, he will give you minimal information. This closes down communication. In this scenario, he would have to decide whether to say yes or no based on what he thought his mother wanted him to say and then he would have stopped talking.

While it is wise to use primarily open-ended questions, there will be times when you need to ask a closed-ended question. The closed-ended question "Did you get a pink slip?" was asked as a way to get information that the parent needed. Closed ended questions usually require a yes or no answer but can also require brief factual statements.

Open-ended questions enhance communication in all areas of parenting. For example, if you want to know how your child is doing on a school assignment, rather than ask, "Did you finish your book today?." use an open-ended question such as "Tell me how the book began. What happened next? What did you like best and why?" Rather than "Did you work on your report?," ask, "Tell me several things you discussed in your report." If you rephrase what he tells you, he will know you are listening and, therefore, he will be more inclined to continue sharing information with you. An open-ended question, such as, "Tell me about this picture you colored," is more likely to elicit a discussion than a closed-ended question, such as, "What color is this?" When your child returns home from a sports event or music event, ask open-ended questions such as, "What are some of the things you are learning about ball handling?" or "What did the music director do and say to encourage everyone to practice? What else did she say?"

Using open-ended questions gets you information now and promotes a positive, long-term relationship with your child. They will encourage him to openly share his thoughts with you. It is so easy for a parent's questions to squelch a child's thinking and discourage future sharing of experiences. To avoid this, make certain your questions stimulate thinking.

On the other hand, interrogation stops communication. Interrogation, which parents hope will enable them to get to the bottom of a problem, may, instead, make it more difficult to get an accurate picture of what happened. It also has an unintended side effect: it creates an adversarial relationship. Interrogation works for the television interviewer, policeman, and lawyer, because they have no interest in a positive, long-term relationship with the person they are interrogating. Their goal is to inflame emotions and, thereby, increase the likelihood that the person may respond before thinking. In contrast, you, as a parent, want to encourage thinking and want a positive, long-term relationship with your child. If you interrogate your child, you may get the information you're looking for this time, but it will cause your child to withhold information in the future. In the preceding example, the mom's initial thought was, "What did he do wrong?" Had she interrogated him, he probably would have been less forthcoming with what happened. In the future, he would not have shared his problems. Since interrogation has little or no long-term positive results, it should either not be used or used very sparingly.

Asking focus questions can make your child aware of important and relevant information. Your questions will help your child determine what factors are highly relevant, somewhat relevant, or not relevant. Relevant information will affect a person's decision. In the previous example, questions focused the child's attention on the bus driver's responsibility and the parent's responsibility. When you use focus questions, you are also modeling how he should approach future problems.

The questions you ask reveal your values. In the previous example, questions emphasized the family's values of thinking and of understanding others. The mother took care not to stymie the child's thinking skills. Since this parent felt the walk to the corner was good exercise and knew the home on the corner let the children stand inside when the weather was bad, she did not feel the bus stop's location was harmful. In addition, she actively promoted good child-school relationships. The parent limits her discussions with the school to issues with long-range implications for her child. This was not one of them.

Advance your child's level of thinking by using questions

Questions can also be examined based on the level of thinking required to answer them. On Path 1 you were told there would be times when you need to combine parenting techniques. This is one of them. You will find it beneficial to combine what you are now learning about questions that influence your child's level of thinking with each of the many parenting tasks that includes asking questions.

The questions listed below, based on the revised Bloom's Taxonomy, start with the type of question that requires an easy answer and progress to questions that require more complex thinking to answers. You do not need to start with a level-one question or ask your child a question at each level. Start with the level you feel your child can answer easily. You can always go up or down in your level of questioning. Responses always show the ability to do the previous steps. He can't understand the meaning of what you said (level 2) unless he also heard your words (level 1). He can't evaluate the situation (level 6) unless he is able to do all the preceding five levels of thinking. The questions listed below start with the type of question that requires an easy response and progresses to questions that require more complex answers:

- Level 1: "Tell me what I just said" lets children repeat your words and, thus, lets you know that they heard your words.
- Level 2: "In your own words, tell me what I just said" eliminates a parroting of what you said as an acceptable response. By using their own words or by explaining what you said, they demonstrate that they understand what you said.
- Level 3: "Give me an example of ____" requires them to think of a way to apply or use the information you discussed. Applying

or using information requires more thinking than just having to remember what you said.

- Level 4: "What do you need to consider?" requires that they understand the complexity of the concept. It also requires them to know, understand, and apply all the previous levels of thinking.
- Level 5: "What else could you do?" requires your children to come up with a new idea (i.e., extend their thinking). They have to utilize the previous levels of thinking and review what they know from other situations.
- Level 6: "What questions will you ask yourself the next time you need to find a solution?" This will enable you to understand how your children evaluate ideas and requires them to use all of the previously mentioned levels.

It is very easy to get into the habit of just asking questions that determine whether your child is listening to you, but it is essential to also ask questions that will expand her thinking. By selecting questions that require your child to do more complex thinking, you will greatly enhance her ability to think abstractly. Questions are powerful parenting tools. Use questions that stimulate communication and thinking.

Use a thinking chair

Since both time-out (discussed on Path 8) and the thinking chair (which will be discussed now) require sending your child to a chair or a special location, these approaches may, at first glance, appear to be the same. But their similarity ends with being sent to a chair. The thinking chair and time-out are based on different psychological principles and parent actions; thus, they will have different outcomes. In time-out your child is removed from an activity that he is enjoying, returns after a specified length of time and you do no or little talking. With the thinking chair, your child may, or may not, be enjoying the activity. You give your child a task to do that will help him think about his behavior and do not let him leave the chair or area until you have discussed the situation with him. Requiring him to reflect on his behavior helps him understand his role in what happened and how to avoid similar problems in the future. Your older child can do this by writing down his responses to your questions. A younger child will need to draw pictures of his ideas. For example, he could draw or write about:

- This incident and why his behavior was not appropriate;
- Fun things the offending children have previously done together;
- Fun things they could do together in the future;
- Ways to handle a similar situation in the future.

By calling the chair a thinking chair, you let your child know that the rules are different from the ones you have for time-out. The success of this approach rests on your ability to clearly tell your child what she is to do and your ability to maximize your child's learning during the follow-up discussion. At that time, you must remain calm, be an active listener, and use questions that promote thinking. If either you or your child cannot remain calm, you may want to revert back to time-out.

You can use the thinking chair even when you are not at home. For example, you can do this while waiting to get in to see the doctor or when you are dining out. Say, "Your chair is now a thinking chair. I want you to write three sentences (or draw a picture) that show how your behavior is affecting those around us and three sentences (or pictures) about what you are going to do now." When the task is completed, the two of you can discuss the picture or what was written.

The thinking chair has many advantages. You can use this approach to teach your child how to analyze a social situation so he can avoid future conflicts or—if the conflict does reoccur—a better way to deal with it. But, if you are having a problem controlling your anger or your child is too emotional to draw a picture or write a narrative, time-out will be the more effective approach. If your child is having trouble expressing himself verbally or understanding what you say to him, use time-out. Be honest about yourself and your child's needs.

Teach How to Deal with Others

Negotiate success

Negotiation is not capitulating to your child's wishes. It is a preemptive attempt to avoid conflict. Giving in to whining is a lack of consistency. Negotiation does not mean arguing with your child. Arguing means you are forgetting that you are the parent and that you are letting your child control the interaction. Negotiation is a way to teach your basic goals, illustrate how to apply them, and learn how to make appropriate decisions when you are not around to guide your child's decision making.

Not every decision is negotiable. Your basic values are *not* negotiable, but they can be explained as you negotiate with your child. On the other hand, your decision regarding a specific situation may be determined by special considerations that can be negotiated. For example, when is it permissible (or not) to eat Halloween candy, to go to a friend's home, or to have a sleepover? Make it *very, very clear* from the onset whether a specific situation is negotiable. If your child asks permission to do something that is negotiable, initiate the conversation by asking a question such as, "What do you think about that idea?" or "What do you suggest?" If it is not negotiable, just clearly state your decision and then tell your child, "This decision is not negotiable." End of discussion. Identify situations that are negotiable by asking him questions that invite his input. If you don't establish a way to identify what is negotiable, you will find your child challenging every decision you make.

Negotiation does not mean manipulating your child to come to your conclusion. For example, are you willing to be flexible as to the length of time and the amount of money he can spend at the amusement park, or have you already decided how long he can go and how much he can spend? If you have already decided those factors, then this situation is not negotiable. In that case, just tell your child your decision and explain the reasons for your decision. On the other hand, if you are flexible as to the amount of time and money available for this event and are willing to factor in his thoughts on those matters in order to come to a joint decision, then this situation can be used to teach negotiation.

Negotiation means finding a win-win solution. The way you handle conflicts, or potential conflicts, models, for your child, how to handle conflict in general. The trick is to turn a potential problem into a learning situation. When your child makes a request and you are uncertain whether or not to grant it, you and your child can gather the information needed to make the decision. You can teach her how to listen and express her ideas respectfully. By modeling the flexibility and compromise necessary to create a win-win situation, you can show your child how to become a successful negotiator.

Some negotiable events occur in normal living. For example, do you consider his weekend bedtimes negotiable? Both parties involved should suggest a revised bedtime and the reasons they feel that time is appropriate.

Negotiated decisions are helpful for two reasons. First, your child is more likely to accept and implement negotiated decisions than parent-imposed decisions. Second, your child will approach future decision making in a similar fashion. If you model this approach each time it is appropriate, your child will learn how you make wise decisions. While initially time-consuming, it saves a lot of time later.

Promote problem-solving skills

I observed a skilled preschool teacher model problem-solving techniques as she helped her class of four-year-olds find a solution to a problem.

SCENARIO

A group of four-year-olds was getting into a circle on the floor in anticipation of story time. Madison and Latisha were trying to squeeze into the same spot. Madison shoved Latisha out of the way. Before Madison could get into the spot, Ashley, who had been standing quietly just behind them, slipped into the coveted spot on the floor. From across the room, Mrs. K heard loud, angry voices, all calling to her at the same time.

Madison: Mrs. K, Ashley took my spot.

Latisha: No, that's my spot.

Madison and Latisha argued over who got to sit next to Mackenzie. Ashley sat quietly, hoping that her skill of slipping in while the others fought would get her the coveted seat, but Randy noticed her and loudly described the situation to Mrs. K.

Mrs. K: Three people want to sit there. Can three of you sit in that spot?

Madison, Latisha, and Ashley: No.

Mrs. K: What should we do?

Ashley: pointing to the other side of the circle: Madison and Latisha can sit in one of the empty spots over there.

Madison: I can sit here now, and Ashley can sit by Mackenzie next story time.

Mrs. K.: Madison suggested taking turns. Do you like that idea?

Latisha: It's not fair for Madison to be first.

Mrs. K.: How could we decide?
Suggestions came from the children who were observing:
You could pick, Mrs. K. Or you could think of a number and
whoever guesses it could sit there. Or the person who got there
first could sit there today.
Mrs. K: Who was the first to get there?
Latisha: I did.
Madison: I did.
Ashley: I sat down first!
Latisha: Only because Madison pushed me.
Mrs. K: Each of you feels you have a claim on this place.
Randy (who was sitting on Mackenzie's other side): Someone
can sit on this side.
Mrs. K: How many places do we have now?
Several classroom children: Two.
Mrs. K: Is that enough?
The children agreed that there were not enough spaces.
Mrs. K: What can we do?
Mackenzie: I could sit by Madison at lunch.
Mrs. K: Ashley and Latisha could sit by her now, and Madison
at lunch. Do you think that is a good idea?
Latisha: I want to sit with Mackenzie at lunch. Madison, you
and Ashley sit here now.
Mrs. K: Ashley and Madison can sit here now, and Mackenzie
and Latisha can sit together at lunch. Do you like that idea?
Everyone agreed. Mrs. K asked each child individually if she
liked that idea. All nodded and said yes.
Mrs. K read the story.

Problem-solving studies show that the first solution is rarely the best solution. It takes time and a nonjudgmental reaction to suggestions to unblock our preconceived ideas and free us to come up with a better solution. The teacher in the previous scenario did just that. She provided the time her students needed to suggest various solutions, she noted each solution but did not evaluate it, and she avoided questions designed to get the "right" answer. It is highly unlikely that either the teacher or the children had the final solution in mind when the discussion began.

The solution in this scenario and other real-life situations is rarely one that comes to mind quickly.

When you began reading the situation, it is highly probable that you wondered why the teacher didn't ask Madison and Latisha to find another place to sit, since Ashley was already sitting there, or make all three students find a different seat, since they were fighting over it. That would have solved the problem quickly. You may have told yourself that the teacher wasted valuable teaching time. Determining where the children would sit was not the goal. The goal was to model conflict resolution using problem-solving skills. She could have scheduled a problem-solving lesson, but an artificial problem-solving task would not have provided as valuable a learning opportunity as this real situation. Most of the children stopped what they were doing and gathered around to see what was going to happen. The observers learned that the fighting children had many ideas and were able to come up with a solution to their problem. They heard some ideas that were rejected. They listened to the reasons the other children gave for the possible solutions. Finally, one was accepted. What a great example of taking advantage of a teachable moment.

There will be ample opportunities for you to teach problem solving. Watch for times your child is having a problem selecting between two or more alternatives. Your child may be overextended and need to decide which of her activities to drop. Your child may need to select what to take on a trip. She may even be debating on which of several projects to do for science. Problem solving, like negotiation, isn't manipulating your child so she will come to the decision you want. If the decision is truly hers, promote her problem-solving skills by using the following problem-solving steps:

1. Use open-ended questions to stimulate your child to think of various solutions.
2. Create a list of possible solutions. Accept all suggestions without evaluating them.
3. Ask your child to eliminate approaches that will not work.
4. Your child can select the solutions that are the most likely to work and state why he thinks those options might work.
5. Your child can select the best solutions and try them, if that is feasible.

It is imperative that you do not try to direct your child to the answer you want. Rather, use questions that stimulate multiple solutions. Only after he has suggested multiple solutions should you ask your child to evaluate and select the solutions he could try. Remember, rarely is the first idea the best idea. Encourage your child to review and revise his plans. The solution will be more readily acceptable and doable if it comes from your child. Your child needs to be able to problem solve, both now and as an adult.

Resolve conflicts

Arguing. Fighting. Unwilling to share. You feel like screaming, "Stop! Just get along!" Take a deep breath. Calm yourself and remember that you don't always agree with your friends or family. Children, adults, and entire countries all disagree at times. In fact, adults who are unable to come to a mutually agreeable solution often end up in court, where a judge has to intervene. Handling social conflicts is something your child will have to deal with throughout his life.

How you handle your child's conflicts with others will affect his success in handling social conflicts with his siblings and peers when you are not around to intervene. Just as adult conflicts may require a court decision, children's conflicts may require the parents to act as judge and jury. Regardless of your child's ability—or inability—to arrive at an amicable solution, your child has experienced the process. With practice, he will need you to act as judge less and less frequently.

You may feel a little less irritated by her conflicts if you approach them as a teaching opportunity. Conflict resolution techniques will:

- Teach your child how to uphold her positions without being confrontational;
- Promote your child's understanding of others' feelings and perceptions;
- Encourage fairness, empathy, and values;
- Discourage your child from instigating problems;
- Teach your child how to be a peacemaker;
- Develop thinking and problem-solving skills.

While problem-solving and negotiating skills are incorporated into conflict resolution, the high emotions and the adversarial nature of conflict will require more adult input and control than you needed to provide in problem solving. You will need to incorporate all the questioning techniques you are learning on this path. You will need to ask questions that stimulate thinking as well questions that require specific levels of thinking (Bloom's levels 1 through 6). Conflict resolution utilizes the following steps:

1. Calm yourself. Avoid jumping to conclusions. Things may not be like they seem at first glance.

2. De-escalate the conflict. Calm the children. Assure each child that he or she will have an opportunity to be heard.

3. Listen to the speaker and praise the listener(s). Let one child speak at a time. Inform them that good listening is the most important part of resolving the conflict and that you and they are going to be attentive listeners. Don't interrupt or let the other children interrupt. Praise the children who are listening and assure them that they also will have an opportunity to speak without being interrupted. You could say, "I want to hear what each of you has to say, and I can only do that when one person is talking. You don't need to agree with the speaker, but you do need to understand how he perceives the situation." Ask the listener(s) to tell you what the speaker said (Level 1 questions). Assure the listeners that being able to tell you what the speaker said in no way indicates agreement. On the other hand, it does tell you that they are good listeners. Don't evaluate what the speaker said, but tell the listeners that they did an excellent job of telling you what was said. Your goal is to help them articulate (not agree with) the views of others.

4. Have the children switch roles and proceed as in #3.

5. Work with the children to summarize the problem, but don't demand one viewpoint (Level 2 question).
6. Identify areas of agreement and disagreement. Ask the children what is important to them and to the others in the conflict (level 4 question). Keep in mind that there are situations where we, as adults, have to agree to disagree. There are times when intelligent people see things differently, but you can still show respect for each other's opinions.
7. Ask the children for possible solutions (Level 5 question).

Up to now, as the mediator, you have used open-ended questions and several different levels of questions to clarify the points of disagreement and agreement. You have some possible solution. At this point, you will *incorporate* what you previously learned about *problem solving,* such as eliminating and selecting solutions. Hopefully, the group will come up with a possible solution that can be implemented. As a last resort, the adult or parent can act as judge and final decision maker.

Take the time to teach your child how to negotiate, problem solve, and resolve conflict. If your child has experiences in each of those three areas, she will be able to establish positive relationships with her peers and with adults.

Create a "no-lose" environment

This brief discussion of an existing parenting approach will provide additional insight on ways to maximize your child's involvement in decision-making. In his book *Parent Effectiveness Training,* Thomas Gordon urges parents to use a no-lose method of parenting that includes active listening, "I messages," and problem solving. As you listen to your child, Gordon wants you to determine who owns the problem. Does your child own the problem because she has an unmet need or desire? Do you own the problem because your needs are not being met (e.g., you can't complete your tasks)? Or has the problem occurred because of a relationship issue, such as a conflict between children or between your children and you?

The approach that Gordon recommends depends on who owns the problem. If your child owns the problem, Gordon advises you to use the already discussed skill of active listening. If you, the parent, own the problem, send an "I message." For example, you could say, "I just got home from work, and I am very tired. I need to rest for a few minutes." You are letting your child know that the problem is due to your need for rest and not because of something he has done. You cannot disguise a "you message" by starting it with "I feel." Saying, "I feel angry because you did not let me rest" is really a "you message" that means "You made me angry." "You messages" create conflict and do not solve problems. "I messages" contain a nonjudgmental description of the problem, express how the problem affects you and how you feel about the problem.

Gordon's book also states that if the problem is a relationship problem, avoid a win-lose approach and instead use a no-lose approach. The no-lose approach involves finding a mutually acceptable solution. There are six steps to the no-lose method. First, identify and define the con-flict. Second, list alternative solutions. Third, discuss and evaluate the various solutions. Fourth, select the best solution. Fifth, implement the solution. Last, evaluate how well the solution worked. Complete dis-cussion of this open-ended approach can be found in Gordon's book, *Parent Effectiveness Training*.

Promote positive peer interaction

If your child has good social skills, she will have less conflict with you and with others. Your child's social skills develop as she interacts with you and her peers. In most cases, when she is interacting with her peers, your role is to stand back and let her solve her own problems. This allows her to experience the natural consequences of her behavior and to become more self-reliant. You will need to intervene when a child or children are in physical or emotional danger, when the noise level or physical confrontations are escalating, or when a conflict is between children with unequal power due to age, size, or temperament.

You can increase your child's ability to solve her own problems by carefully selecting the other children you invite over to play. Don't invite a best-friend duo to come play, as loyalty to one's best friend is particularly strong among girls. Another girl trying to become a friend with one or both of the girls in a best-friend relationship is often viewed as a threat to the earlier relationship. In order to maintain the existing support system, best friends often reject all "outside" attempts of friendship.

If you decide to invite someone over to play, invite a child that is close to your child's age and temperament. This will allow you to step back and let social learning develop naturally. Since social interaction with one person is less complex than social interaction with two children, start with the least complex interaction—that is, start by inviting over just one friend. Be sure that age appropriate toys or crafts are easily accessible. When conflicts develop, step back and observe your child. In most cases, she will solve her own problems. Intervene only if emotional or physical safety demands it. Success with others and being part of a group increases social confidence and reduces the likelihood that she will become a victim of bullying.

Promote positive interaction with authority figures

If you let your child control (or bully) you, he will also be disrespectful to other adults. Do not let him kick you or hit you. If he does, firmly grasp his hands and tell him, "I do not like that." Tell him how you want him to get your attention or let you know he is angry. Tell him, "Stand quietly by me, and I will ask you what you want." When you teach your child how to talk respectfully to you, you are preparing him to talk respectfully to other authority figures in his life (e.g., teachers and scout leaders).

Encourage your child to have a positive attitude toward his teacher and school. Don't complain about your child's teachers in front of her. If she has a problem with a teacher, listen to her and encourage her to find a solution. Use the problem-solving approach that I explained earlier to help her come up with possible ways to deal with the situation. As your child interacts with his many teachers, each one with his or her own personality, he will learn how to deal successfully with the various bosses he will have during his adult life.

You have learned many ways to prevent parenting problems and to maximize your parenting control and to develop your child's self-control.

Path 10

Support Your Child's Emerging Abilities

Your child's abilities emerge rapidly. By the time she is five years old, her brain has reached 90 percent of its adult weight. This significant growth makes these years important ones for learning. Of course, this does not mean you should try to accelerate her learning. It also does not mean you should use flash cards to teach your baby to read or push her to use the potty before she is physically ready. Reading and potty training will come, but earlier is not necessarily better. Pushing your child to develop these skills and other skills before she is ready may cause her to fall behind later. Likewise, failing to provide her with an environment that supports emerging skills is also harmful to your child. You stimulate your baby's, toddler's and preschooler's brain cells when you provide her hands-on experiences that involve integrating several senses.

You stimulate your older child's thinking when you discuss local and world events, model reading, and take trips that expand her awareness of the world. You are your child's first and most important teacher!

Provide a Springboard to Success

Whenever there was a new program promoting early reading or promising to increase a child's intelligence, someone usually asked what I thought of it. I was not shown any that I regarded as useful. If you want to provide your child a springboard to success, teach her to be a responsible member of your home. She will then become a responsible member of her classroom and society in general. You do need to provide age-appropriate and developmentally appropriate experiences to support her emerging abilities. On this path I will describe those emerging skills and explain the importance of seizing teachable moments to enhance them.

Seize the teachable moments

Many unplanned learning opportunities (teachable moments) occur as you and your child live your lives together. You are seizing a teachable moment when, as explained earlier, you teach your baby the words for body parts and clothing as you dress and bathe her. Seizable moments also include giving her age-appropriate household chores, such as cooking, which will teach reading as she reads the recipe and math as she measures the ingredients. Mealtimes are great times for conversations, which promote language development and social skills. If you spend considerable time chauffeuring your child from one activity to another, limit your time on the cell phone so you can use those teachable moments to encourage her to share what is going on in her life. Since your life with your child is rich with seize-the-teachable-moment opportunities (unplanned learning opportunities), there is no need for formal teaching or using flash cards.

Don't let technology based games cause you to overlook the value of board games and card games. When you and your child are playing an age-appropriate board game or card games, use their built-in teaching value such as turn taking, memory building (remembering the rules, etc.), visual discrimination (needed for reading), talking, and listening. When your child is a preschooler, you can select games like Candy Land and progress to chess and other more demanding games as he matures.

Parroting the parent

Whether you do or do not want to be, you are your child's grammar teacher! He will use the same phrases and words you use. If you curse, so will your child. If you use correct grammar, so will your child. If you use verbs incorrectly, he will do likewise. Your child will learn language by parroting those around him.

Listen to your child when he is playing or talking with friends. This will provide feedback on how you are doing as his language teacher. He will use your tone of voice, your grammar, and your vocabulary. If you like what you hear, congratulate yourself. If not, start modeling the type of language you want him to use. There is no way you can teach him what you want without modeling it first. Unfortunately, there is no parenting technique that will keep your child from doing what you do.

Artwork by Anna

Read it again!

Before a child can be successful in reading, she must learn that reading brings joy, so read frequently and with expression. She needs to know how to hold a book and go from the front of the book to the back. She also needs to acquire the skill of sitting and focusing. There are so many things your child needs to learn before you teach her that c-a-t stands for cat.

Don't waste your time using flash cards with your infant or pre-schoolers. Do use the language activities described on earlier paths, as well as the following ones:

1. Read age-appropriate books. Let your baby chew on the cloth book and your preschool child turn the pages. Read the same story over and over so she can "read" it back to you. Continue reading to your children throughout their elementary-school years. Make reading fun.

2. Teach your preschool child to pay attention to sounds. Have your child listen for sounds in his environment. He will need to listen for various letter sounds in the words he will be learning to read.

3. Talk to your child. His ability to understand what you say will develop more rapidly than his ability to express his thoughts.

4. Listen to your child. Being an active listener will increase his desire to talk; he needs to practice expressing his thoughts.

5. Read poems and help your child find the rhyming words. Help your child discover that words, which sound the same at the end, also look alike at the end (e.g., "ran" and "can").

6. Help your child discover that words, which sound the same at the beginning, also look alike at the beginning (e.g., "ball" and "baby").

7. Call attention to visual details by asking your child to look for specific items in a room or to describe a picture.
8. Play memory games. Your child will need to remember how words look (i.e., build a sight vocabulary).
9. Have your child "read" to you. When he retells a story from the pictures, he is practicing reading.
10. Act out or illustrate a story or a book. This requires him to understand and remembers what the book said. This promotes comprehension, which is the most difficult part of reading.
11. Write down stories he dictates to you. This helps him connect spoken and written words. Have him read the story to you.
12. Label the items in your child's room. This teaches your child that a collection of letters stands for a specific item.

If you provide your child the activities listed previously, he will understand the reading process and, therefore, will learn to read and comprehend what he reads better than those preschoolers who went through a workbook-based learn-to-read program. Once his reading skills emerge, there are things you can do to support those skills:

- Continue to read to your elementary-age child.
- Read the same stories or books that your child is reading so you can discuss them.
- Encourage him to read aloud to you and others. Read the same story back to him, so he can hear how it sounds when it is read smoothly and with expression.
- Establish a time each day to read.
- Model reading by reading books that you enjoy.

Countdown to success in math

Teaching math using daily experiences makes learning math more enjoyable and meaningful than using workbooks or flashcards. A child who sees math primarily as a school subject that requires memorization is going to be less interested in math than a child who sees math as a useful tool in daily life. Prepare your child for success in math by teach the following preschool math concepts:

1. Identify and name shapes like circle and squares that you see around your home (pre-geometry skill).
2. Rote counting is saying number names in order (i. e., one, two, three). It does not demonstrate an understanding of number values (e.g., the amount meant by the numbers one or five). Since children learn names early and rote counting relies on memory and not abstract thinking, rote counting is learned at an early age.
3. Classification is putting things together in groups. First classify items by one criterion (e.g., put socks in the sock drawer). Next, classify items by two criteria like yellow and ball. This requires him to find the right toy in the right color i.e., a yellow ball. Gradually increase the number of criteria he must use.
4. One-to-one correspondence is placing objects on top of or next to each other to show that both groups have the same number of items. Have your child help you set the table and ask her to put one spoon by each plate. Then ask her if there are the same number of spoons as plates.
5. Number value requires your child to understand that the number two indicates a *group* of two items, and the number five indicates a *group* of five items. I have observed three year old children

258

correctly count out five blocks, but when asked, "How many blocks are there?," respond with a random amount instead of five. After all, why would the child call the group of blocks by the *name he gave to the last block*? If you say, "Put your markers, crayons, and paper in the box," you don't refer to all the items as "paper." Why should he use the number name he gave to the last block to refer to all the items?

Number value requires your child to look at the objects as a group. For example, after counting out two pieces of candy, put them both in your child's hand and have her squeeze the candy. Then say, "You have two pieces of candy." Your child comes perfectly formed for learning the number two. Compare her two feet, hands, and ears to her one nose, tongue, and head. At this point, she will probably understand one, two, and more than two (i.e., lots). After she learns two, teach her three. Count out three spoons. Say, "I have three spoons in this hand." Teaching three will take time, but your child will probably learn four and five quickly. At this point she will understand how to determine number values and will apply this principle to larger groupings.

6. Relationship concepts require your child to shows how items or groupings relate to each other. For example, teach big or small, few or many, and more or less.

7. Ask your child to stack blocks to create a group of one (one block), a group of two (a stack of two blocks), then a group of three, and so on. This helps your child see how a group of five items relates to groups of four or six items.

8. Word problems are hard for most people, so expose your child to word problems that arise in your daily life. Ask questions like,

"How many plates are on the table? How many more do we need?" By providing real-life word problems that require active thinking and hands-on responses, you are helping prepare her for the abstract word problems she will face later.

If you provide the experiences listed previously, your child will be better prepared to learn math in the elementary grades.

Ask "Why?"

It is your turn to ask "why?" It's a great way to teach science to your child. If you have a pet, discuss what it needs and why. Growing a plant is great fun and will teach your child how to care for a plant. Science, just as with reading and math, is best taught through your daily activities.

There is no one your child is more interested in than himself; therefore, teach him how to care for himself. Teaching your child about food and exercise is imperative, given the increase in obesity throughout America. Good eating habits start by providing your child with good food choices in your home. Look through magazines and cut out pictures of good, healthy foods. Paste them on a sheet of paper, and it will become a grocery list you can take when you go shopping. Put healthy snacks where he can reach them and teach him your rules regarding eating snacks.

Teach him that some things, like medicines, are consumed only as needed, and some things, such as cleaning supplies and drugs, are never put in our mouths. Keep potentially dangerous items where your child cannot reach them. You will need to teach your elementary-age child the dangers of both prescription and illegal drugs. You are the most influential person in your child's life so talk to him about drugs while he is still in the elementary grades.

Encourage exercising. Unfortunately, very few children live where they can play outside unsupervised. Your child needs as much fresh air and exercise as you did, but she is probably enticed by the television and other technological devices to just sit. Both of you will benefit from taking a bike ride or taking the dog for a walk. You can buy technology games that require your child to move in order to play them. Teach her that exercise has a positive effect on her strength, endurance, emotional balance, and mental development. Home is the place to teach her respect for and the science of caring for her body.

Explore your home and beyond

Your preschool child's social studies will focus on your family and the interdependency of family members. If you have a weekly chart or calendar that shows each person's responsibilities, use that as a visual reminder of your interdependence. Dress-up hats and clothing lets your preschool child pretend to be Mom, Dad, or community helper. As your child enters elementary school, he can learn about his community, nation, and the world. Help him draw a map from his house to a friend's home. Take your children on trips to zoos, museums, or large department stores. Visits to grandparents' houses can provide them with a new perspective. Vacations taken to various parts of our country, historical places, or national parks are also great learning experiences. If you live life with a variety of experiences and have conversations about them, you will give your children a head start in life.

Artwork by Rachel

I think I can; I think I can; I know I can

Motivation is vital for success. The "I know I can" person, like the "I think I can" train, tries even though he is fearful. The possibility of success spurs one forward. The other side of "I think I can" is the realization that failure is possible. With the realization that failure is possible, many children do not try. So why, in the face of possible failure, do some children try and others do not?

They try, because when they faced a difficult but doable task, they were repeatedly given just enough support to be successful. If you provide your child with little or no support, and she frequently fails, she will stop trying (i.e., she will have low motivation). If your child's efforts never come up to your standards, and you redo or improve what she felt was a completed project, she will stop trying. For example, the parent who trims the jagged edges of her three-year-old's project so it will look neat or retypes her child's third-grade paper is telling her child that her efforts aren't good enough. Rather than cutting the shape for your three-year-old, you can hold the paper firmly so she can experience the success of being able to cut on the line. Your third grader can ask for help with some of the computer commands, but she needs to feel the success that comes from completing the class assignment by herself.

Think back to how you taught a multistep task in the section "Step up to success" on Path 8. You made certain that your child was successful before you moved on to another step. This created an "I can" attitude. When you taught your child to negotiate, problem-solve, and resolve conflicts, you were teaching self-reliance and creating an "I can" attitude. When you taught him ways to deal with peers, you were developing an "I can" attitude. Experiences that provide just enough support for success and enough independence for your child to feel he did it himself produce motivation.

It is also important to help your child to see the relationship between his decisions and the consequences of his actions. If he is made aware of the relationship between what he does and what happens, he will learn that he can cause something to happen. Accusatory questions lead to feelings of helplessness and self-doubt. Questions, which promote an understanding of how one's actions contribute to either success or failure, create goal-oriented behaviors; i.e., motivation. Likewise, if success is considered the result of luck, and failure means you are unlucky, he will be less likely to try in the future; i.e., become an unmotivated person.

Motivation stems from moderate support when trying new things and nonjudgmental questions that allow your child to see the relationship between his behaviors and their consequences. Motivation is one of the human characteristics most affected by environment.

Expand Your Child's Learning Opportunities

Carefully select a child-care program

Parents who work outside the home for personal or financial reasons need to rest assured that a *good* day care program provides children with security and a good beginning in life. When selecting a day care center, ask the following questions:

- "How long has each of your teachers been here?" If teacher turn-over is high, there must be a reason that those who can leave do. Run; don't walk. If teachers stay in their positions for multiple years, your children will have the continuity of care they need.
- "Are you licensed?" Licensing is a must, but it deals only with the most *basic* safety needs and provides no information about the center's quality.

- "What is the education level of each of the teachers?" Teachers' education will affect their decisions; their decisions will determine the quality of your children's experiences. A two- or four-year degree in early childhood education or child-care is a must.
- "Is the school or day care center accredited by the National Association for the Education of Young Children (NAEYC), your state's NAEYC association, or other recognized professional organization?" Unfortunately, accreditation is not required, and very few centers go through the accreditation process. If your children's potential facility is accredited, count yourself fortunate to have an outside organization that has verified its quality. Please keep in mind, however, that not all quality centers go through accreditation.
- "Is the director and are the teachers members of NAEYC or other professional organizations that provide educational workshops?"
- "Do the teachers and the director attend the in-service workshops professional teacher organizations provide in your state? What do they do to upgrade their skills?"
- Ask to see their curriculum and a sample lesson plan. It must be activity-based (play, manipulative toys, art experiences, and dramatic play) and provide sequential, hands-on, developmentally appropriate learning experiences (refer to the previously listed activities parents should provide). Worksheets or workbooks must not drive their lesson plans. Your children should not be required to sit for hours in front of a TV. Keep in mind that the day care teachers are your co-teachers, and you want them to develop your children's skills as we have previously discussed along this path.

- Ask for the discipline plan. It should be focused on positive behaviors and rewards.
- What is the child-to-adult ratio? Check your state's requirements. Common ratios are 1:4 for infants, 1:5 for young toddlers, and 1:10 for three to four year olds and 1:20 for five year olds.
- Review the center's health policies and plans for dealing with a sick child. There must be a place for the sick child to lie down while he waits for you.
- Do they provide nutritious snacks and meals?
- Ask for payment costs and a payment schedule.

Observe your child's potential classroom. Watch the teachers interact with the children. Ask for the names and phone numbers of parents in your child's classes. Of course, the facility will need to obtain permission from those parents before providing you with their contact information or names. When you speak with them, ask them specific questions rather than a general question, such as, "Do you like the center?" You can also ask them to describe an activity their children did last week or how a child's illness was handled. You can also ask them what they like best and what they would like to see changed and why.

Good early experiences require time for children to play, color, paint, run, make cookies, work on puzzles, climb, and generally explore their world. Your child needs an adult who understands child development and how to promote good social, emotional, and cognitive development. Children need an adult who seizes teachable moments. They can get all those things at home or in a day care setting.

Do your homework. Select a good day care center and then relax knowing you have a parenting partner. Studies have shown that children who attend quality day care centers do as well in school and in social situations as those who are cared for in a home.

Be a double advocate: The parent-school connection

Whether your child is attending a preschool or an elementary school, you are your child's best advocate. You also need to be the school's best advocate. If your child sees the school through the eyes of a pro-school parent, she will view what happens at school in a positive light. If you share significant information about your child with her teachers and seek information from them about your child, the school will perceive you as a concerned, supportive parent and will view your child in a more positive light. By being both pro-child and pro-school, you can help both be more productive.

Don't run to the school and complain every time things don't go your child's way. First, do active listening. Your child may solve her own problems, or you may learn that this specific situation will resolve itself. That is the best outcome for your child.

If you do go to the school, *your purpose should be to gather information*. Studies on perception show that humans filter their sensory input (i.e., what they see and hear) through the lens of their own experience. You will filter what you hear from your child through the lens of your own school experiences, what you believe about your child, and your view of the teacher and the school. That may or may not be accurate for this situation. When you go to your child's school you will probably hear views that are different from yours and your child's. That does not mean that either your child or the school isn't telling the truth. Children and adults often see things differently.

Start by asking the teacher to describe your child's academic progress and social interactions. You need to know the teacher's perspectives, especially if they are different from yours. Listen respectfully. This will increase the likelihood that the teacher will listen to you. Don't attack the teacher's descriptions of your child, but do describe specific incidents that present your child in a different but positive light.

Listen with an open mind. All decisions need to be made jointly with the school. As a person who is aware of varying perceptions, you will anticipate multiple views. Your goal will be to gather these different views as a way to get a more accurate picture of the school and your child. Proving that your child is right or wrong is pointless. If the school and your child see things differently, try to understand both views. Use the problem-solving techniques you learned earlier. By serving as an advocate for both the child and the school, the school and your home will be able to move in unison.

Reflections on homeschooling

The number of parents who have decided to home school their children has increased dramatically the past few years. Some parents have become disillusioned with public school curriculums and policies. Others feel that homeschooling will enable their child to learn the required information in less time, thus allowing him time to pursue special interests. Some parents feel their child is capable of more advanced learning or require more specialized help than he will receive in a group setting. Others want to assure that their values are being taught. The reasons for homeschooling are as diverse as the parents and children involved.

If you decide to home school your child, be sure you set aside a specific time and location in your home for this activity. Like any good teacher, you must be prepared and have goals. You must include active learning and not just rely on workbooks. You must also learn your state's requirements for homeschooling and meet or exceed them. You need to learn what support services you school district provides and make use of them. In addition, the Internet provides curriculums you can follow and classes your children can take. Charter schools, developed to support homeschooling, can provide homeschooled children with valuable learning experiences in subject matters where the parent lacks expertise and with experiences learning in a group setting.

You must also provide your homeschooled children with opportunities for social interactions. Some homeschooling parents join together for field trips, school parties, and other events. You can also receive help from local and national homeschooling organizations.

Don't make the decision to home school lightly. Talk to parents who have chosen a public school, private school or a religious-based school and ask them why they made that choice. A private school or a religious-based school may teach values similar to yours and meet other needs of your child. It takes teaching skills, time, and commitment to successfully home school. Be sure your decision is based on your children's needs.

Rebuff that bully!

Your child's best protection against bullying is a good defense. Use all the information learned on earlier paths to promote a positive self-image and to learn how to deal with others. The bully is looking for someone who looks like a victim. The more you build your child's positive self-image, the less likely a bully will see her as a victim. Her strong verbal and negotiating skills can also give her confidence when facing a bully and reduce the likelihood that he will select her to bully.

Having friends reduces the likelihood that your child will be perceived as someone to be bully; therefore, use what you learned earlier about creating positive peer interactions to help her develop friends. A bully often selects someone who has few or no friends; the bully does not want someone to come forward and stand up for the victim or to go get help.

Teach your child how to distinguish between accurate and inaccurate social feedback. Just as you don't use a wavy mirror to determine how you look or whether you need to comb your hair, you don't allow a bully to tell you who you are. In the same way that your reflection is unreliable in a wavy mirror, a bully's reflection is distorted. Teach your child that she, not the bully, is in charge of her feelings and behaviors.

Bullying gives the perpetrators a feeling of power. Children frequently identify with and look up to those they perceive as powerful and, therefore, when they see how scared a child is and the power the bully gains over others, they join the bully's group. Thus the bully gains status. Other children are often afraid to stand up for the victim for fear of becoming the next victim themselves. Bullies often look for locations with minimal adult supervision such as the school bus, the path home, or the school playground to decrease the likelihood that they will be caught.

Bullying must not be ignored. Children who are harassed and endure years of being taunted are more inclined to use alcohol and drugs in high school. They often become antisocial and aggressive. If you think your child may be a victim of bullying, use open-ended questions and active listening to encourage him to talk about it. Learn who his friends are - who he sits with at lunch and on the bus and what he does during recess. Help him develop friendships with other students. If possible, remove him from the group where he is bullied and help establish a group of new friends who are similar in age and temperament. Listen carefully to your child. The emotional pain he is experiencing is great and real. You will need to do reflective listening and role-playing. You may need to talk to his teacher, scout leader, or group director—depending on where the bullying occurs.

Not only is being bullied harmful to a child, so is *being* a bully. It is not in a child's best interest to become a bully. If someone tells you that your child has bullied another child, don't ignore or deny it. Calmly ask your child about the situation. Ask your child what happened and how he feels about the incident. Ask him how he thinks the bullied child might describe the incident and how he thinks the victim felt. Then ask your child how he will act toward the victim in the future. Listen carefully and repeat his key points to let him know you are listening. Discuss the characteristics of leadership and how they are the opposite of bullying. Discuss the behavior you expect from your child in the future. Maintain contact with the school about the situation, and have strict guidelines and consequences. Ask yourself why your child feels a need to victimize others and determine what parenting changes will help your child develop more appropriate social interactions.

Anyone can become the victim of a bully. Develop a plan with your child's teacher or the school psychologist. You need to help your child develop new behaviors, whether he is doing the bullying or being bullied.

Along this path you have learned how to maximize your child's success. You have not tried to force her to become the person you envisioned but have been sensitive to her strengths and have enabled her to meet her own potential.

Artwork by Anna

Path 11

Avoid Obstacles that Clutter Your Parenting Path

Create a Balanced Life

Speak up: There is just one of me!

It's not just your child who creates challenges and makes demands on you; so does life in general! You heralded your new baby's arrival by calling grandparents, aunts, uncles, and friends. As she grows, joy is replaced by stress. The demands of work and home can be crushing. Trying to keep a roof over your baby's head and diapers on her behind can squelch what began joyously. Your toddler goes through the "terrible twos." Your elementary-age child tattles continually. You may find yourself needing to help your aging parent. The realities of life set in. You discover that the paths through parenting are full of obstacles that cause you to stumble or fall.

Prioritizing is essential for good parenting and personal survival. Also, look for allies in parenting. Your extended family, neighbors, friends, community groups, and church organizations can assist you. Remember, it is important to take care of yourself.

Balance the needs of each individual and the total family

Each person in your family—your spouse, older child(ren), and younger child(ren)—has unique needs and interests. The challenge of family life is to balance all these needs. The task of creating a family requires respect for each person, including respect for yourself. If you give all the attention to your children, your marriage will suffer, and your children will become self-centered. A good marriage is a great gift to your child. The order shouldn't be children first and parents second, nor should it be parents first and children second. You are a family unit. You are the one with the experience and thinking skills to determine which needs are paramount at any given time.

You also need to balance your children's needs. If one child receives all the attention because of age or special needs, balance among them is lost. Although a new infant requires extensive amounts of time, it is imperative to schedule time for the other children as well.

You, not your extended family, make the rules for your children. At the same time, you can encourage grandparents, aunts, and uncles to be a viable part of the children's lives. Having support from extended family expands your children's experiences with different personalities and increases their feelings of security. Extended family members often relish and hope for involvement in your children's lives.

Balance all your jobs—both inside and outside your home

All parents are working parents. Raising children is a job. This is true whether you are a stay-at-home parent, a work-at-home parent, or you are employed outside your home. The parent who chooses to stay home with his or her children has chosen an important and demanding profession. The parenting profession requires problem solving, organization, stamina, and knowledge. Although more moms than dads are the stay-at-home parents, we are seeing more stay-at-home dads than we did in previous years.

The need for time management escalates if, in addition to your parenting job, you also have a job outside the home. Some employers are more family-friendly than others. Both parents need to learn what options their employers provide when children are sick, need to be taken to a doctor, or if some other emergency develops. You may also explore flextime or the option of working from home. Finding quality childcare is imperative. In spite of all the demands made on you, it is imperative that you and your children have enjoyable time together.

Seek support from friends and family

Friends, our family of choice, are a great source of emotional and physical support. Having a friend requires being a friend. Sharing carpooling and childcare can provide mutual support and can reduce stress for all parents involved. For childcare sharing to be successful, there must be an equitable exchange of childcare and the parents involved should share similar views on child rearing.

When developing an ongoing support system that includes children spending time in each other's homes, I found that it was more important that the parents have similar rules and parenting techniques than it was for the children to be friends. When both parents used similar parenting techniques, our children became friends over time; but when my children felt the other parent was unfair or had rules they didn't understand, shared child care didn't work.

Networking with other parents can ease your stress. When my children were in elementary school, I participated in a collaborative summer program that they and I enjoyed. The program began each summer with a planning meeting that included the four mothers involved in the program and our seven children. Each mother was responsible for one week of activities for each child in the program. Thus the program consisted of seven weeks of activities, plus a culminating event. Anticipating upcoming events and preparing for the activities at their homes eliminated the children's complaints of boredom. Mothers enjoyed their free time knowing that their children were happy and learning. The activities were varied and included making a film, creating an inflatable shark, presenting plays, putting on a Mexican fiesta for their families, creating art projects, and much more. One of our end-of-the-year field trips involved a train trip to a historical site. We spent the summer following the children's last year in elementary school organizing, publicizing, and running a one-day fundraising carnival. Some years, the summers ended with the dads in charge of the kids and the moms spending the weekend at a hotel where we could talk, laugh, and have a great time! To this day, my adult children tell me that they have happy memories of those summers.

Mothers of Preschoolers (MOPS) groups encourage Christian parenting, provide informative lectures, and do creative crafts. These busy moms support each other in times of joy and need. If you have preschool-age children, expand your friendships by calling your local churches to learn which ones sponsor a MOPS group in your community. I loved the years I spent as a mentor mom for a MOPS group. Seeing young mothers' commitments to their children gave me confidence in the future.

Positive social relationships can sustain you when life seems overwhelming. Developing and maintaining friendships takes time and effort, but doing so creates a balanced life and brings great rewards for both you and your children.

Make healthy decisions

Nutrition impacts all you do. You know that balanced nutrition is vital, but it is very enticing to take advantage of the fast-food restaurants where you can buy food your children will eat without complaining. Don't compromise on nutrition. Grocery stores are stocking more washed fruits and vegetables and partly prepared or easy-to-prepare foods. Even fast-food restaurants are now enabling you to limit your children's food choices to more nutritious side items, drinks, and grilled meats. Your children may complain if you limit their choices to nutritious offerings, but their health will improve, and they will learn to make wise food choices. Buy healthy foods. Your family needs foods from all the food groups and a time to sit down and eat together. Don't skimp on eating together around the family table!

Exercise is imperative. I was amazed to learn that exercise, rather than making me tired, gave me energy. Walking is excellent and needs no equipment. Weight lifting is highly recommended for both men and women, because it protects your bones and tones your bodies. Water exercises reduce joint stress. Tennis, yoga, and other exercise programs may fit your interest. Find an exercise you like. As a parent, you need the strength, endurance, and energy that you get from exercise.

Parenting is demanding, and to properly meet those demands, you must be healthy and rested. Napping when your child naps is not being lazy; it's smart. If you plan to get all your work done and then rest, you will never get any rest. There is no end to parenting demands. You must plan for yourself.

How many times have you or a friend said, "I don't have time to get sick." If you eat a balanced diet, get adequate rest, and exercise regularly, you will get sick less often. When you do get sick, your children will probably be solicitous and helpful. Use this time to teach empathy. A healthy, rested parent can focus on parenting and make wiser decisions. You owe it, not only to yourself, but also to your children to take care of yourself.

Remember—if a parent isn't happy, no one is happy

Take care of yourself. Keep in mind that the airline attendants tell passengers to first adjust their own air masks and then assist others. They know that if you run out of oxygen, you will not be able to help anyone. Likewise, if you run out of emotional energy, you will not be able to meet the demands of parenting.

You wear many relationship hats—a spouse, a mother, a father, a daughter, a son, a sibling—but you are more than just a relationship. You are a person with adult interests, hobbies, and goals. Finding time for them is challenging. Get a babysitter and go out with friends or have a date night with your spouse.

Enjoy your hobbies. Include your children whenever possible. If you like scrapbooking, your children can make one too. If you like to do art projects, provide age-appropriate art materials for your children. If you are musical, you and your children can make music together.

What are your life's goals? Don't give them up. If your children see you as a goal seeker, they will also be goal seekers. Although goals are sought over a lifetime, you can take little steps in the direction of your goals. Little steps can add up to big steps over time. Giving up who you are is self-destructive.

Balancing often requires looking at your life over an extended time. For example, when planning a balanced diet, you do not plan a breakfast that includes something from each of the food groups. Rather, you plan to eat something that fits in each area of those food groups sometime during the day. When you are balancing your life, you may decide that what *you* want now is to spend more time with your children, because they are not going to be around fifteen to twenty years from now. You may choose to focus on hobbies or get an advanced degree later. There is a time and a season for all things, but maybe not all at one time. Living a balanced life is something you will accomplish over your lifetime.

Keep Abreast of Advances in Technology

Select television programs that teach your values

The television can be your friend or foe. It can motivate your children to dance and sing or put them into a trance. It can teach them about the world and encourage acceptance of others, or it can model violence and inappropriate language. It all depends on which programs you permit your child to watch. You must set guidelines. You can record programs suitable only for your older child that she can watch after the younger child goes to bed. To maximize the benefit of television, watch it with her and use the program's contents to teach her. For example, when watching a sports program, don't zone out with a beer in your hand. Ask your child to predict what might happen or discuss what makes a given player an all-star. Use these moments to motivate your child to go outside and practice that sport. National Geographic programs, history programs, and educational television are also available. Just because a program is advertised as a children's television program does not automatically make it appropriate. Some children's programs are very violent. Just as your child will select junk food over nutritious food, left on his own, your child will select junk television over educational television. You need to guide your child's television viewing.

How much time should you permit your child to spend watching television or engaged with technology toys? You can decide based on how your child has spent that day. Has he had some vigorous activity today? If not, any time is too much. Provide him with a physical activity instead. Have you read him a story or two or has he read to himself? If not, have him read. The attention-grabbing nature of technologically is a two-edged sword. It can maintain your child's attention long enough for him to learn. However, it can also become addictive and thus reduce involvement in other valuable activities.

Two hours of inappropriate television is two hours too many. On days when your child has been active mentally, physically, and crea-tively, and there is a program that will benefit her, by all means, let your child have more television time. If a specific show or sports event is a family event and includes visiting and interacting, then be sure to include your child, even if she has already used up her allotted televi-sion time.

Is it bad to use television as a babysitter? Usually, but not always. Television is not the only activity that will keep your child engaged while you pursue necessary tasks. A creative center with paper, mark-ers, and other simple art materials, or a reading center with readily accessible books, would be a preferred "babysitter." Rather than putting your child in front of the television set while you do your daily chores, include him. Of course, if an emergency comes up, it is better to have the television occupy his time than to have him wander off into danger.

If you have a task that needs to be done immediately, you can be flexible and let him watch television. Now, if you tend to have "emergencies" once or twice a day, then you need to reschedule your tasks. But if an emergency develops and you use the television to keep your children safe, don't beat up on yourself. It's the frequent use of television as a babysitter that is problematic.

Control the use of technology

The ease with which your child navigates the Internet not only prepares him for our computer-run society, but it also places him in danger. Provide guidelines for the use of the computer, keep the computer in a room frequented by all family members, and ask questions about his computer use (e.g., "What websites do you visit?").

There are obstacles and blessings along the path of parenting. Your child's smiles and hugs make parenting efforts worthwhile. Your balanced life will give you the stability you need to not trip over obstacles along your parenting path. Take care of yourself! Enjoy your children!

Path 12

Create Your Parenting Plan

Dear Parent,

In the introduction, I stated that the goal of this book is to empower you to be the best parent that you can be. You will make mistakes. Admit them, forgive yourself, and move on.

I want you to use your adult thinking skills and what you have learned in this book to develop your personal parenting plan. Here are some things you should consider as you make your personal parenting plan:

- Some of the approaches are suitable for young children, and some are just for older children.
- Some of the approaches are suitable for children with limited vocabularies, and some require extensive vocabularies.

- Some of the approaches are useful for preventing problems, and some are useful for responding to your children's inappropriate behaviors.
- Some approaches are necessary only when you need to respond firmly and expect immediate compliance.
- Others teach respect for authority and obedience.
- Many approaches teach family values.
- Some teach thinking skills like decision-making and problem solving.
- Some enable your children to develop self-control.
- Some encourage your children to become motivated people.
- And, of course, all of these approaches require that you exercise self-control and judgment.

You are now ready to create your personal parenting plan.

Your friend and fellow parent,

Ruth Ann

Write your Plan

Filling in the following boxes will focus your thinking on the multiple factors involved in good parenting and help you develop your personal parenting plan. If you have more than 2 children, add boxes for each child. You may write in this book or on separate paper.

Bases of our Parenting (Paths 1 and 3)

Parenting Considerations	Mom	Dad
Preferred Parenting Style (Path 1)		
Your Values (Path 1)		
Your Rules (Paths 1 and 6) Rules should grow out of your values and be useful in many situations.		

Temperament (Path 3)

Discuss how your temperaments *interact*)

Mom	Dad	Child 1, age___	Child 2, age ___

Appropriate Responses Plan (Paths 4 through 8)

Parenting Considerations	Child 1, age _____	Child 2, age ____
Age-typical behaviors for children the age of your child (Path 4)		
Your unique child's – temperament, behaviors, and needs (Paths 3)		
Steps you will take to prevent and reduce problems (Paths 5 and 6)		
Appropriate responses to your child's *appropriate* behaviors (Path 6)		
Appropriate responses to your child's *inappropriate* behaviors (Paths 7 and 8)		

Develop a Competent Child (Paths 9 and 10)

Parenting Considerations	Child 1, age _____	Child 2, age_____
Develop thinking and problem solving skills (Path 9)		
Develop academic success (Path 10)		
Develop social competency: - reduce peer conflict - reduce sibling conflict - develop a bully-defense (Paths 4, 5, 7, 9)		
Develop self-control and decision making skills (Path 9)		
Promote motivation (Path 10)		

Supporting Our Child(ren)'s Emerging Abilities (Path 3 and 10)

Parenting Considerations	Child 1, age _____	Child 2, age_____
Special interests and abilities (Paths 3 and 10)		
Steps we will take to support our child's interests and abilities Path 3 and 10		

There is just one of me! Share responsibilities. (Path 11)

Mom will:	Dad will:	Together we will:
Seek help from family and friends (often mutual help):		
Tasks we will hire others to do		

Bibliography

Ainsworth, M. D. S., M.C. Blehar, E. Waters, and S. Wall. *Patterns of Attachment: A Psychological Study of the Strange Situation.* Hillsdale: Lawrence Erlbaum Associates, 1978.

Anderson, L.W., D.R. Krathwohl, P.W. Airasian, K.A. Cruikshank, R.E. Mayer, P.R. Pintrich, J. Raths, and M.C. Wittrock. *A taxonomy for learning, teaching and assessing: A revision of Bloom's Taxonomy of Educational Objectives.* New York: Longman, 2001.

Baumrind, D. "The influence of parenting style on adolescent competence and substance use," *Journal of Early Adolescence,* 11 (1)1991: 56–95.

Baumrind, D. (1967). "Parenting styles—The four styles of parenting," *Genetic Psychology Monographs,* 75 (1967): 43–88.

Bloom, B. S., M. D. Engethart, E. J. Furst, W. H. Hill, and D. R. Krathwohl. *Taxonomy of educational objectives.* New York: David McKay Co. Inc., 1964.

Chapman, G., and R. Campbell. *The Five Love Languages of Children.* Chicago: Northfield Publishing, 2005.

deCharms, R. *Personal Causation.* New York: Academic Press, 1966.

deCharms, R. *Enhancing Motivation: Changes in the Classroom.* New York: Irving Press, 1967.

Dodson, F. *How to Father.* New York: Signet, 1974.

Faber, J., and E. Mazlish. *How to Talk So Kids Will Listen & Listen So Kids Will Talk.* New York: Scribner, 2012.

Franklin, M. B., and S. S. Barten. *Child Language: A Reader*. New York: Oxford University Press, 1988.

Frost, J. *Supernanny: How to Get the Best from Your Children*. New York: Hyperion, 2005.

Gordon, T. *Parenting Effectiveness Training*. New York: Three Rivers Press, 2000.

Haber, J. *Bullyproof Your Child for Life*. New York: Perigee, 2007.

Hill, W. F. *Principles of Learning*. Sherman Oaks: Alfred Publishing, 1981.

Horsfall, J. *Kids' Silliest Riddles*. New York: Sterling Publishing, 2003.

Johnston, P. *Perspectives on a Grafted Tree: Thoughts for Those Touched by Adoption*. Fort Wayne: Perspective Press, 1983.

Kohn, A. *Beyond Discipline: From Compliance to Community*. Alexandria: Association for Supervision and Curriculum Development Press, 2006.

Phelan, T. *1-2-3 Magic: Effective Discipline for Children 2–12*. Glen Ellyn: Child Management Inc., 2010.

Phillips, J. *The Origins of Intellect: Piaget's Theory*. San Francisco: W. H. Freeman and Company, 1969.

Piaget, J. *Six Psychological Studies*. New York: Random House, 1967.

Runkel, H. *Screamfree Parenting: The Revolutionary Approach to Raising Your Kids by Keeping Your Cool*. New York: Broadway Books, 2007.

Singer, D. G., and T. A. Revenson. *A Piaget Primer: How a Child Thinks*. New York: Plume, 1978.

Skinner, B. F. *Science and Human Behavior.* New York: The Free Press, 1965.

Skinner, B. F. *About Behaviorism.* New York: Random House Inc., 1974.

Turkle, S. *The Second Self: Computers and the Human Spirit.* New York: Simon and Schuster, 1984.

Wadsworth, B. J. *Piaget's Theory of Cognitive and Affective Development.* New York: Longman, 1991.

Made in the USA
San Bernardino, CA
23 August 2013